HAL LEONARD GUITAR METHOD

INCREDIBLE CHORD FINDER

W9-ART-611

SECOND EDITION

Easy-to-Use Guide to Over 1100 Guitar Chords

ISBN 978-0-88188-594-1

HAL•LEONARD®
CORPORATION

7777 W. BLUEMOUND RD. P.O. BOX 13819 MILWAUKEE, WI 53213

Visit Hal Leonard Online at
www.halleonard.com

READING THE CHORD NAMES

Chord symbols used in this book:	Chord names:	Alternate symbols for the same chords:
C	C major	C pure
C6	C sixth	
C7	C seventh	Cdom7
C9	C ninth	
C11	C eleventh	
C11+	C eleventh sharp	C9(♯11)
C13	C thirteenth	
Cmaj7	C major seventh	CM7, C△7
Cmaj9	C major ninth	CM9, C△9
Cmaj11	C major eleventh	CM11, C△11
C7-5	C seventh, flat fifth	C7(♭5)
C7-9	C seventh, flat ninth	C7(♭9)
C7-10	C seventh, flat tenth	C7(♯9)
C7+5	C augmented seventh	C7(♯5)
C9+5	C augmented ninth	C9(♯5)
C7 $^{-9}_{+5}$	C augmented seventh, flat ninth	C7 $^{(♭9)}_{(♯5)}$
C6•9	C sixth, ninth	C$^6_9$, C6/9
C dim.	C diminished	C°
C+5	C augmented	C aug., C(♯5), C+
Csus4	C suspended fourth	C sus.
C7sus4	C seventh, suspended fourth	C7 sus.
Cm	C minor	C-, Cmin
Cm6	C minor sixth	C-6
Cm7	C minor seventh	C-7, Cmin7
Cm9	C minor ninth	C-9
Cm7-5	C minor seventh, flat fifth	Cm7(♭5)
Cm7-9	C minor seventh, flat ninth	Cm7(♭9)
Cm+7	C minor, major seventh	Cm(maj. 7)
Cm9+7	C minor ninth, major seventh	Cm9(maj. 7)
Cm+5	C minor, sharp fifth	Cm(♯5)
Cm6•9	C minor sixth, ninth	Cm$^6_9$, Cm6/9

GUITAR CHORD DIAGRAMS

The *Incredible Chord Finder* gives you instant access to over 1100 chord voicings. The top diagram for each chord is the most common voicing, followed by two alternates.

STRINGS

The vertical lines in each diagram represent the six strings of the guitar, with the first string (high E) on the right.

FRETS

The frets are indicated by horizontal lines. If a chord voicing is to be played in an upper position, the fret number will appear in the upper left-hand corner of the diagram. For example, the diagram to the right shows the number 4 in the upper left-hand corner, indicating that the top fret in the diagram corresponds with the 4th fret on the fingerboard.

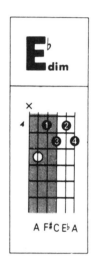

LEFT-HAND FINGERS

The fingers of your left hand are numbered from 1 through 4, starting with your index finger. The numbered black circles graphically show the correct fingering for that chord.

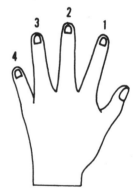

UNPLAYED STRINGS

Strings that are not played are marked with an "X" at the top of the diagram.

OPEN STRINGS

Strings with neither a black circle nor an "X" are played open. (For example: the 1st and 3rd strings of the C chord are played open).

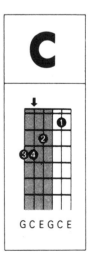

3

BARRING

The figure ⌒ indicates that several strings are "barred," or held down simultaneously with the finger shown. The C7 diagram on the right shows the first finger barring all six strings behind the third fret.

NOTE NAMES

The letter at the bottom of each string names the individual notes of that particular chord.

FINDING THE ROOT

The black circle on the string indicated by an arrow shows the root of the chord. In diagrams where there is no arrow, the root is shown by a white circle.

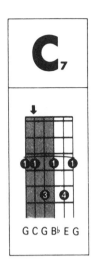

4

BASS CHORD DIAGRAMS

The *Incredible Chord Finder* can also be used by bass players. When using a diagram to find an electric bass note, refer to the four bottom strings in the shaded part of the diagram. These lower strings are the same on guitar and electric bass.

Generally the bass player does not play full chords but must know where the different members of the chord (for example, root, 3rd, or 5th) occur. Any of the notes shown with 6-string fingerings can be played as a bass note at your discretion.

The fingering numbers in the black circles apply basically to the 6-string guitar and can be changed for ease of playing the electric bass.

CONTENTS

C 8

C C₆ C₇ • C₉ C₁₁ C₁₁₊ C₁₃ •

C maj7 C maj9 C maj11 C₇₋₅ • C₇₋₉

C₇₋₁₀ C₇₊₅ C₉₊₅ • C₇₊₅⁻⁹ C₆·₉ C dim

C₊₅ • C sus4 C₇sus4 Cm Cm6 • Cm7 Cm9

Cm7₋₅ Cm7₋₉ • Cm₊₇ Cm9₊₇ Cm₊₅ Cm6·9

D♭C♯ 16

D♭ D♭₆ D♭₇ • D♭₉ D♭₁₁ D♭₁₁₊ D♭₁₃ •

D♭maj7 D♭maj9 D♭maj11 D♭₇₋₅ • D♭₇₋₉ D♭₇₋₁₀

D♭₇₊₅ D♭₉₊₅ • D♭₇₊₅⁻⁹ D♭₆·₉ D♭dim D♭₊₅ •

D♭sus4 D♭₇sus4 D♭m D♭m6 • D♭m7 D♭m9 D♭m7₋₅

D♭m7₋₉ • D♭m₊₇ D♭m9₊₇ D♭m₊₅ D♭m6·9

D 24

D D₆ D₇ • D₉ D₁₁ D₁₁₊ D₁₃ •

Dmaj7 Dmaj9 Dmaj11 D₇₋₅ • D₇₋₉ D₇₋₁₀

D₇₊₅ D₉₊₅ • D₇₊₅⁻⁹ D₆·₉ Ddim D₊₅ •

Dsus4 D₇sus4 Dm Dm6 • Dm7 Dm9 Dm7₋₅

Dm7₋₉ • Dm₊₇ Dm9₊₇ Dm₊₅ Dm6·9

E♭D♯ 32

E♭ E♭₆ E♭₇ • E♭₉ E♭₁₁ E♭₁₁₊ E♭₁₃

E♭maj7 E♭maj9 E♭maj11 E♭₇₋₅ • E♭₇₋₉ E♭₇₋₁₀

E♭₇₊₅ E♭₉₊₅ • E♭₇₊₅⁻⁹ E♭₆·₉ E♭dim E♭₊₅ •

E♭sus4 E♭₇sus4 E♭m E♭m6 • E♭m7 E♭m9 E♭m7₋₅

E♭m7₋₉ • E♭m₊₇ E♭m9₊₇ E♭m₊₅ E♭m6·9

E 40

E E₆ E₇ • E₉ E₁₁ E₁₁₊ E₁₃ •

Emaj7 Emaj9 Emaj11 E₇₋₅ • E₇₋₉ E₇₋₁₀

E₇₊₅ E₉₊₅ • E₇₊₅⁻⁹ E₆·₉ Edim E₊₅ •

Esus4 E₇sus4 Em Em6 • Em7 Em9 Em7₋₅

Em7₋₉ • Em₊₇ Em9₊₇ Em₊₅ Em6·9

F 48

F F₆ F₇ • F₉ F₁₁ F₁₁₊ F₁₃ •

Fmaj7 • Fmaj9 Fmaj11 F₇₋₅ • F₇₋₉ F₇₋₁₀

F₇₊₅ F₉₊₅ • F₇₊₅⁻⁹ F₆·₉ Fdim F₊₅ •

Fsus4 F₇sus4 Fm Fm6 • Fm7 Fm9 Fm₋₅

Fm7₋₉ • Fm₊₇ Fm9₊₇ Fm₊₅ Fm6·9

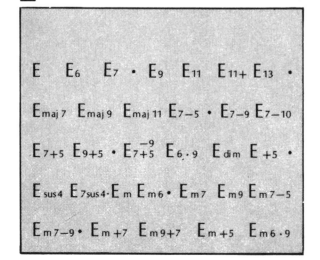
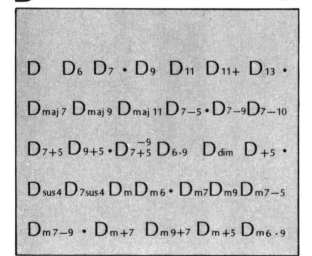

G♭ F♯ 56

$G^\flat$ $G^\flat_6$ $G^\flat_7$ • $G^\flat_9$ $G^\flat_{11}$ $G^\flat_{11+}$ $G^\flat_{13}$ •

$G^\flat_{maj7}$ $G^\flat_{maj9}$ $G^\flat_{maj11}$ $G^\flat_{7-5}$ • $G^\flat_{7-9}$ $G^\flat_{7-10}$

$G^\flat_{7+5}$ $G^\flat_{9+5}$ • $G^\flat_{7+5}{}^{-9}$ $G^\flat_{6\cdot9}$ $G^\flat_{dim}$ $G^\flat_{+5}$ •

$G^\flat_{sus4}$ $G^\flat_{7sus4}$ $G^\flat_m$ $G^\flat_{m6}$ • $G^\flat_{m7}$ $G^\flat_{m9}$ $G^\flat_{m7-5}$

$G^\flat_{m7-9}$ • $G^\flat_{m+7}$ $G^\flat_{m9+7}$ $G^\flat_{m+5}$ $G^\flat_{m6\cdot9}$

G 64

G G_6 G_7 • G_9 G_{11} G_{11+} G_{13} •

G_{maj7} G_{maj9} G_{maj11} G_{7-5} • G_{7-9} G_{7-10}

G_{7+5} G_{9+5} • $G_{7+5}{}^{-9}$ $G_{6\cdot9}$ G_{dim} G_{+5} •

G_{sus4} G_{7sus4} G_m G_{m6} • G_{m7} G_{m9} G_{7-5}

G_{m7-9} • G_{m+7} G_{m9+7} G_{m+5} $G_{m6\cdot9}$

A♭ G♯ 72

$A^\flat$ $A^\flat_6$ $A^\flat_7$ • $A^\flat_9$ $A^\flat_{11}$ $A^\flat_{11+}$ $A^\flat_{13}$ •

$A^\flat_{maj7}$ $A^\flat_{maj9}$ $A^\flat_{maj11}$ $A^\flat_{7-5}$ • $A^\flat_{7-9}$ $A^\flat_{7-10}$

$A^\flat_{7+5}$ $A^\flat_{9+5}$ • $A^\flat_{7+5}{}^{-9}$ $A^\flat_{6\cdot9}$ $A^\flat_{dim}$ $A^\flat_{+5}$ •

$A^\flat_{sus4}$ $A^\flat_{7sus4}$ $A^\flat_m$ $A^\flat_{m6}$ • $A^\flat_{m7}$ $A^\flat_{m9}$ $A^\flat_{m7-5}$

$A^\flat_{m7-9}$ • $A^\flat_{m+7}$ $A^\flat_{m9+7}$ $A^\flat_{m+5}$ $A^\flat_{m6-9}$

A 80

A A_6 A_7 • A_9 A_{11} A_{11+} A_{13} •

A_{maj7} A_{maj9} A_{maj11} A_{7-5} • A_{7-9} A_{7-10}

A_{7+5} A_{9+5} • $A_{7+5}{}^{-9}$ $A_{6\cdot9}$ A_{dim} A_{+5} •

A_{sus4} A_{7sus4} A_m A_{m6} • A_{m7} A_{m9} A_{m7-5}

A_{m7-9} • A_{m+7} A_{m9+7} A_{m+5} $A_{m6\cdot9}$

B♭ A♯ 88

$B^\flat$ $B^\flat_6$ $B^\flat_7$ • $B^\flat_9$ $B^\flat_{11}$ $B^\flat_{11+}$ $B^\flat_{13}$ •

$B^\flat_{maj7}$ $B^\flat_{maj9}$ $B^\flat_{maj11}$ $B^\flat_{7-5}$ • $B^\flat_{7-9}$ $B^\flat_{7-10}$

$B^\flat_{7+5}$ $B^\flat_{9+5}$ • $B^\flat_{7+5}{}^{-9}$ $B^\flat_{6\cdot9}$ $B^\flat_{dim}$ $B^\flat_{+5}$ •

$B^\flat_{sus4}$ $B^\flat_{7sus4}$ $B^\flat_m$ $B^\flat_{m6}$ • $B^\flat_{m7}$ $B^\flat_{m9}$ $B^\flat_{m7-5}$

$B^\flat_{m7-9}$ • $B^\flat_{m+7}$ $B^\flat_{m9+7}$ $B^\flat_{m+5}$ $B^\flat_{m6-9}$

B 96

B B_6 B_7 • B_9 B_{11} B_{11+} B_{13} •

B_{maj7} B_{maj9} B_{maj11} B_{7-5} • B_{7-9} B_{7-10}

B_{7+5} B_{9+5} • $B_{7+5}{}^{-9}$ $B_{6\cdot9}$ B_{dim} B_{+5} •

B_{sus4} B_{7sus4} B_m B_{m6} • B_{m7} B_{m9} B_{m7-5}

B_{m7-9} • B_{m+7} B_{m9+7} B_{m+5} $B_{m6\cdot9}$

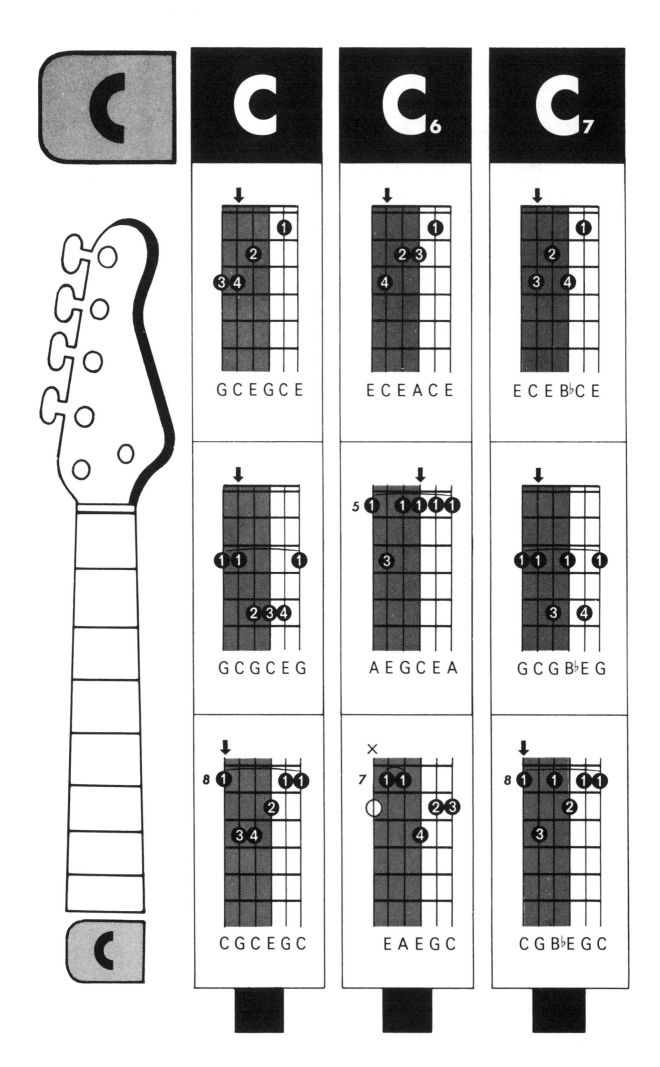

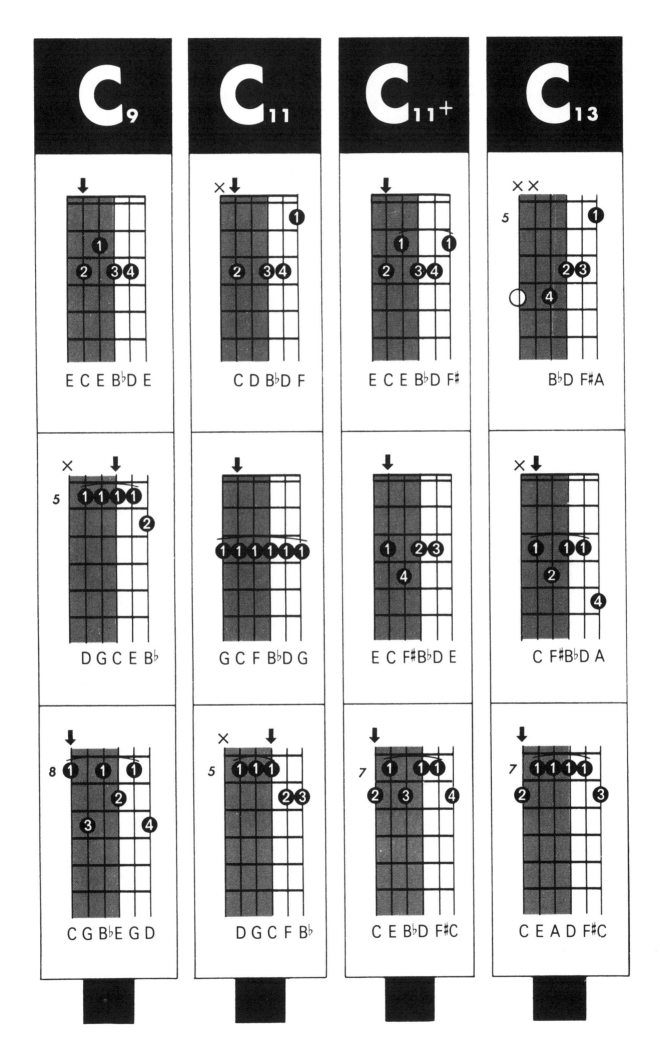

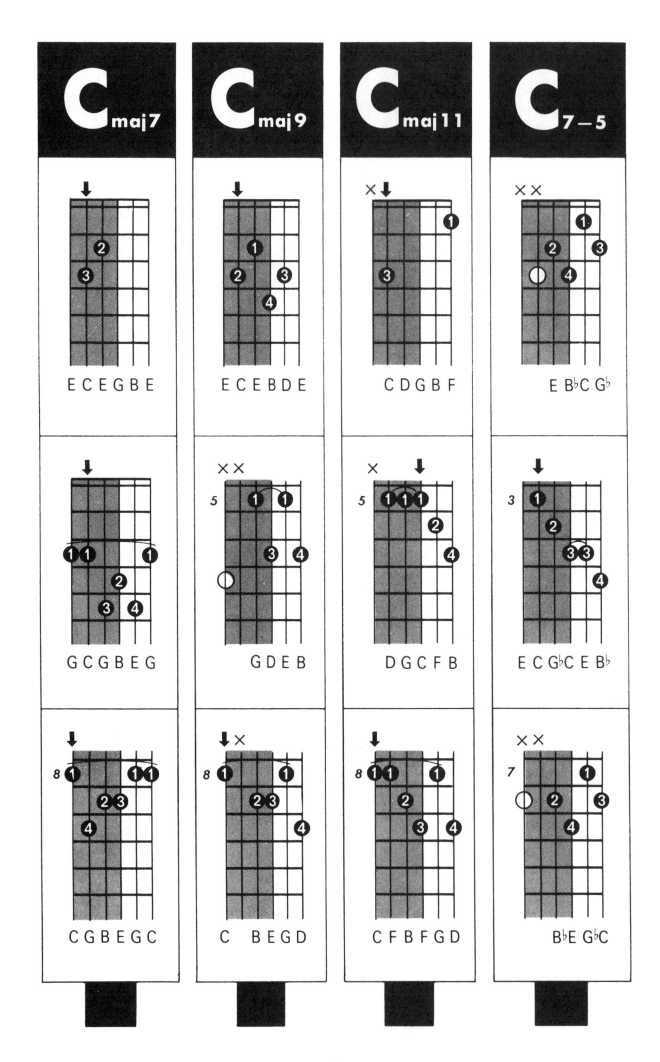

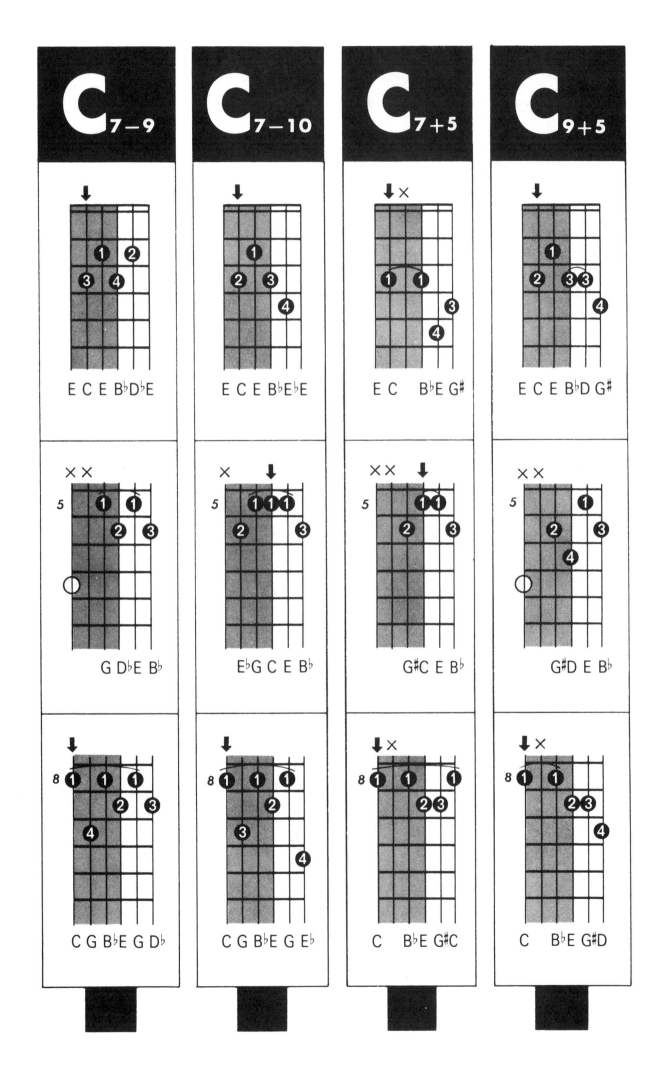

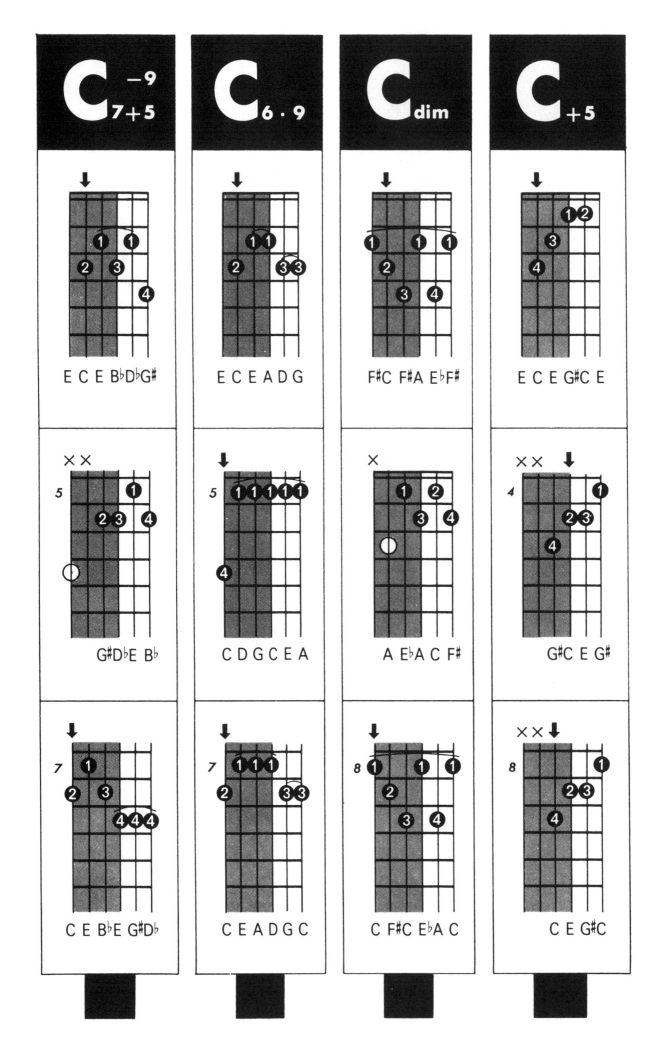

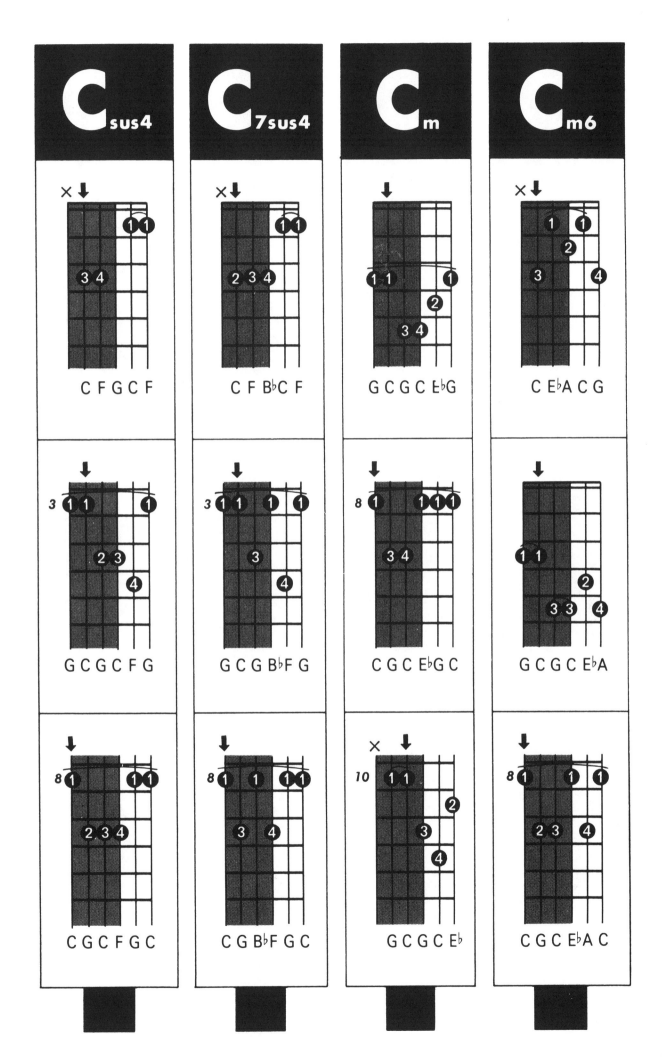

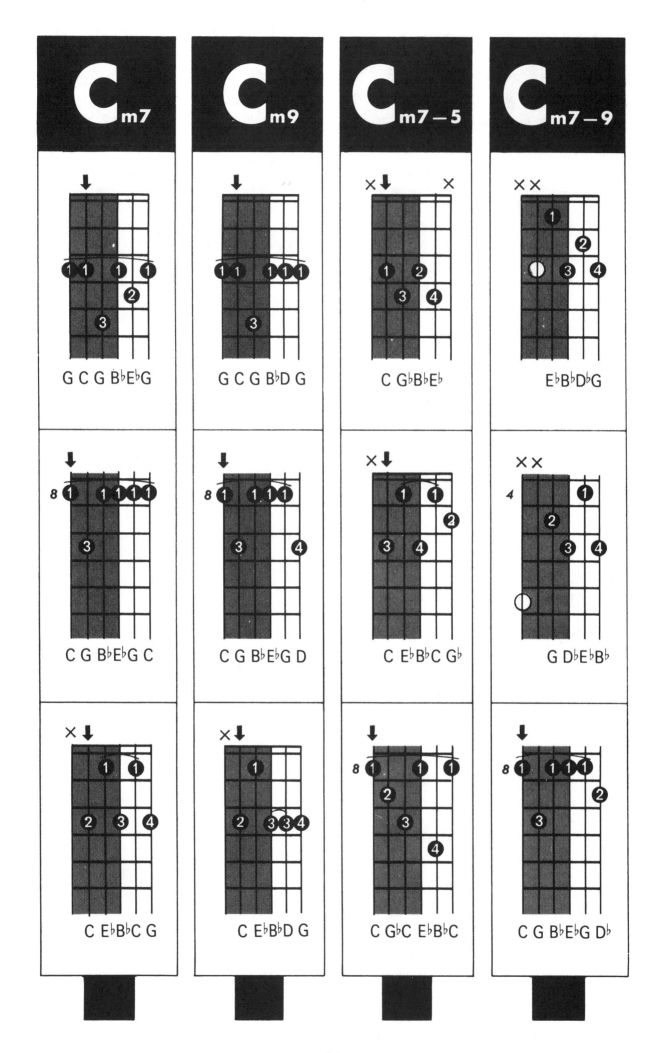

C_{m7}

G C G B♭E♭G

C G B♭E♭G C

C E♭B♭C G

C_{m9}

G C G B♭D G

C G B♭E♭G D

C E♭B♭D G

C_{m7-5}

C G♭B♭E♭

C E♭B♭C G♭

C G♭C E♭B♭C

C_{m7-9}

E♭B♭D♭G

G D♭E♭B♭

C G B♭E♭G D♭

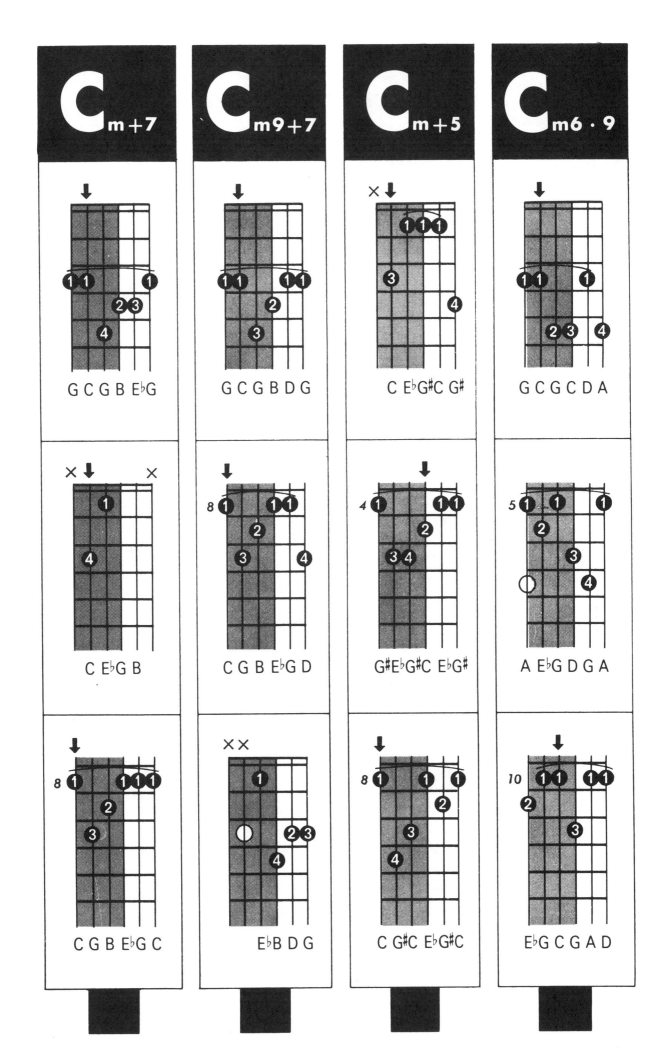

Cm+7

G C G B E♭G

C E♭G B

C G B E♭G C

Cm9+7

G C G B D G

C G B E♭G D

E♭B D G

Cm+5

C E♭G#C G#

G#E♭G#C E♭G#

C G#C E♭G#C

Cm6·9

G C G C D A

A E♭G D G A

E♭G C G A D

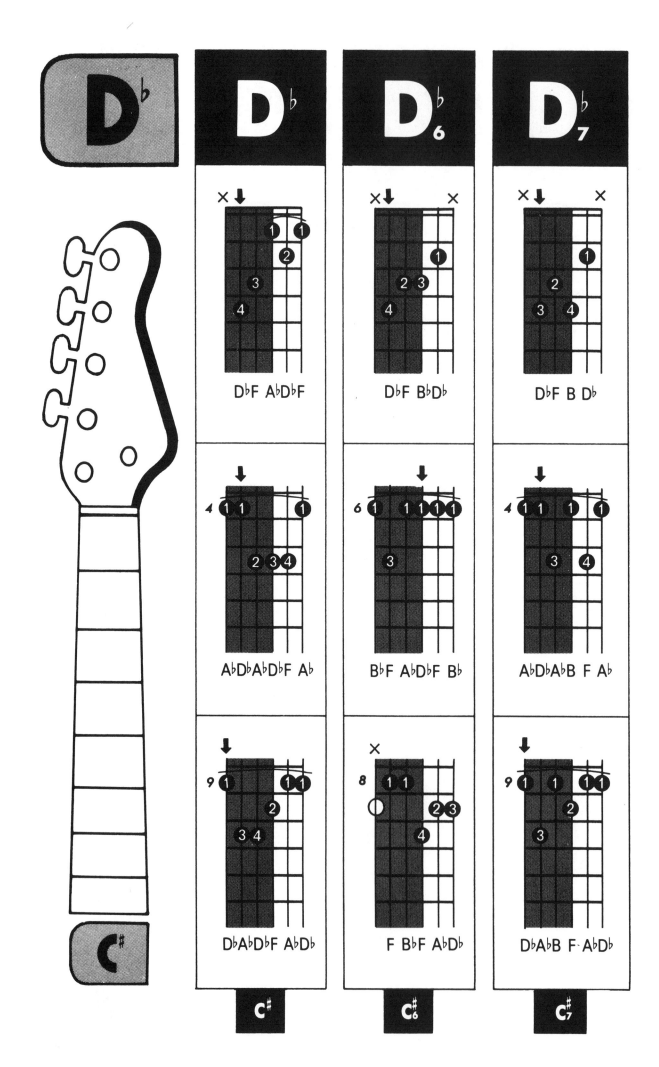

16

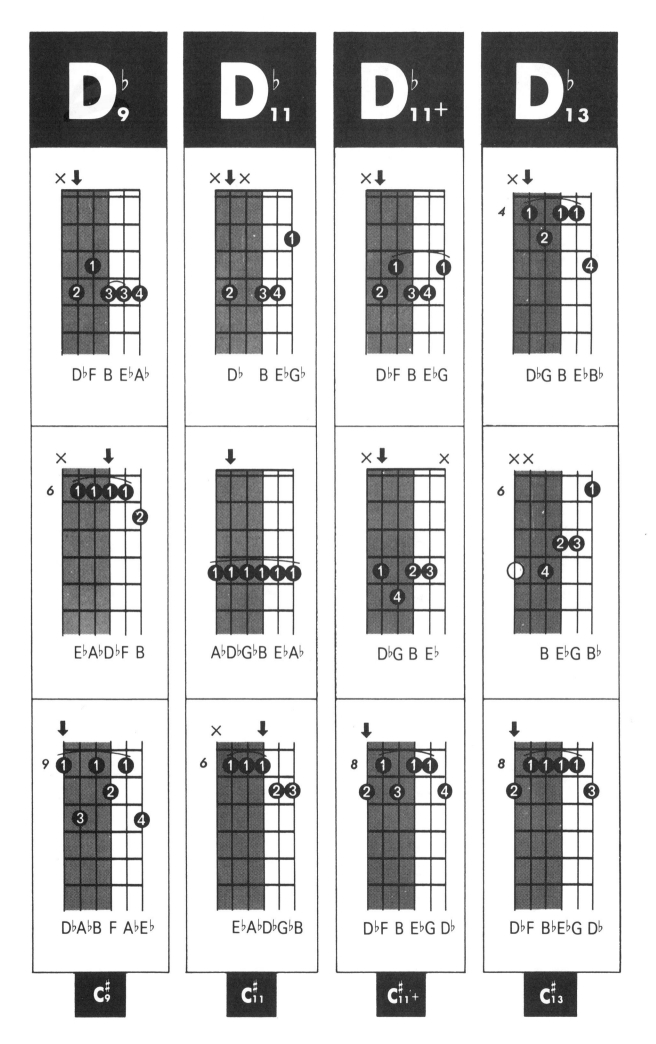

C#

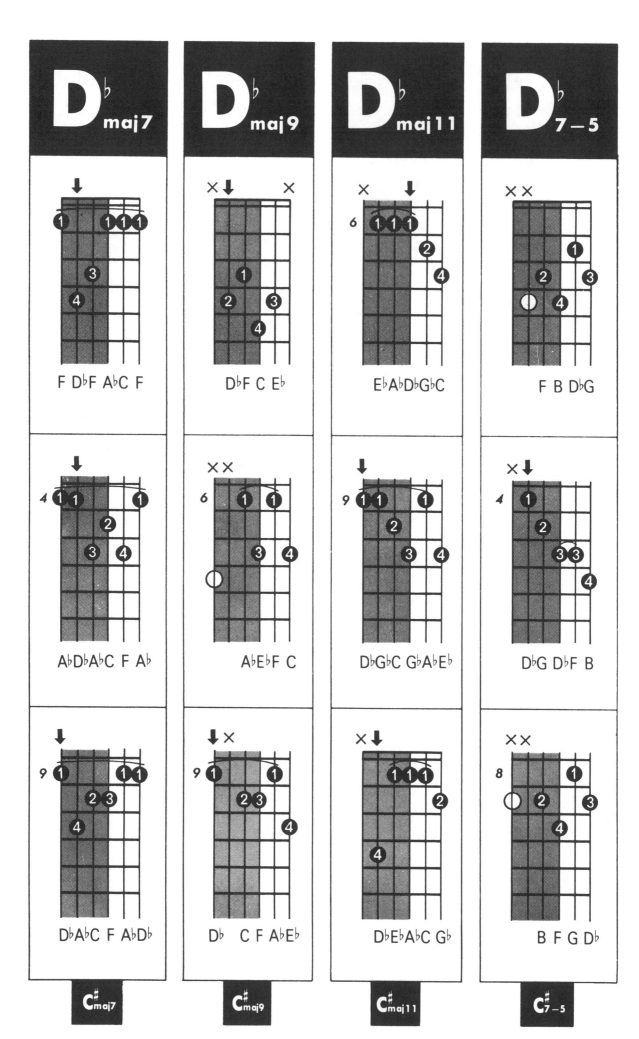

D♭maj7

F D♭F A♭C F

A♭D♭A♭C F A♭

D♭A♭C F A♭D♭

C#maj7

D♭maj9

D♭F C E♭

A♭E♭F C

D♭ C F A♭E♭

C#maj9

D♭maj11

E♭A♭D♭G♭C

D♭G♭C G♭A♭E♭

D♭E♭A♭C G♭

C#maj11

D♭7−5

F B D♭G

D♭G D♭F B

B F G D♭

C#7−5

18

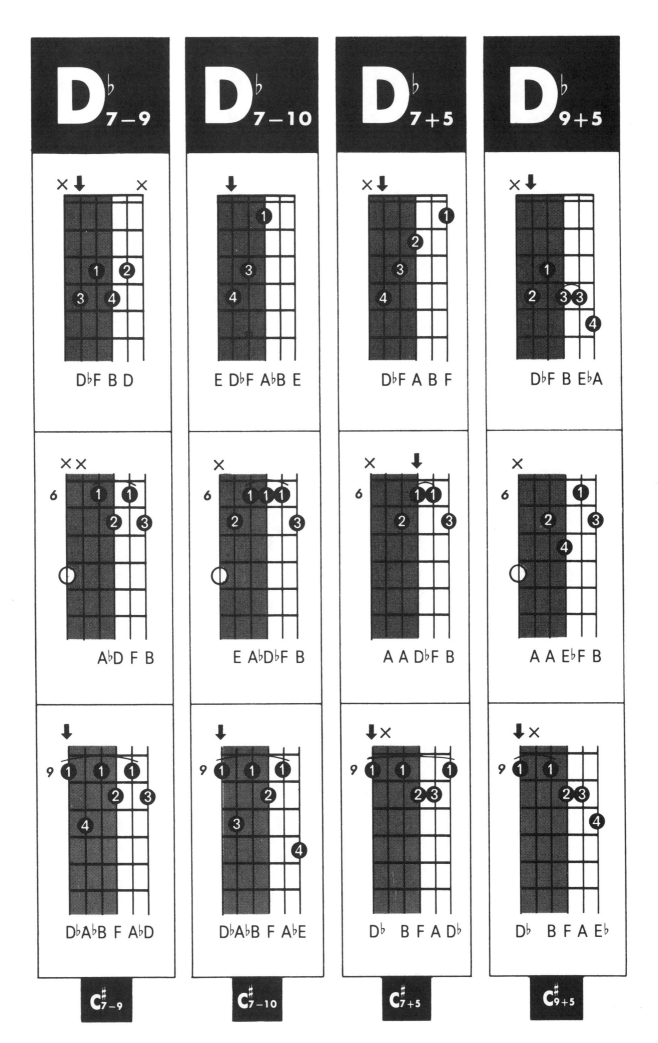

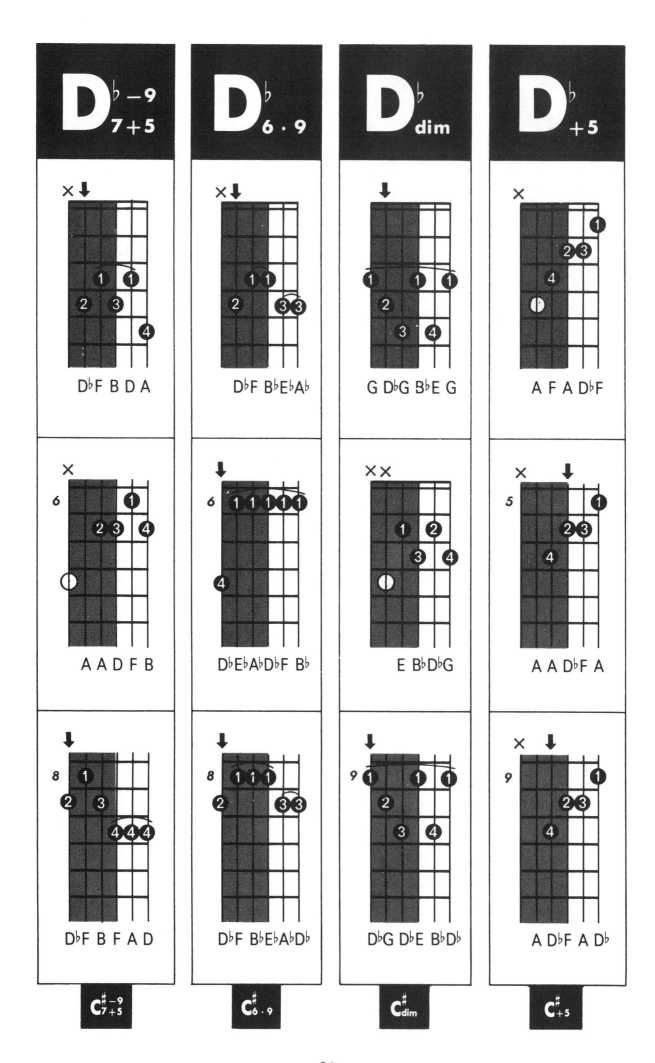

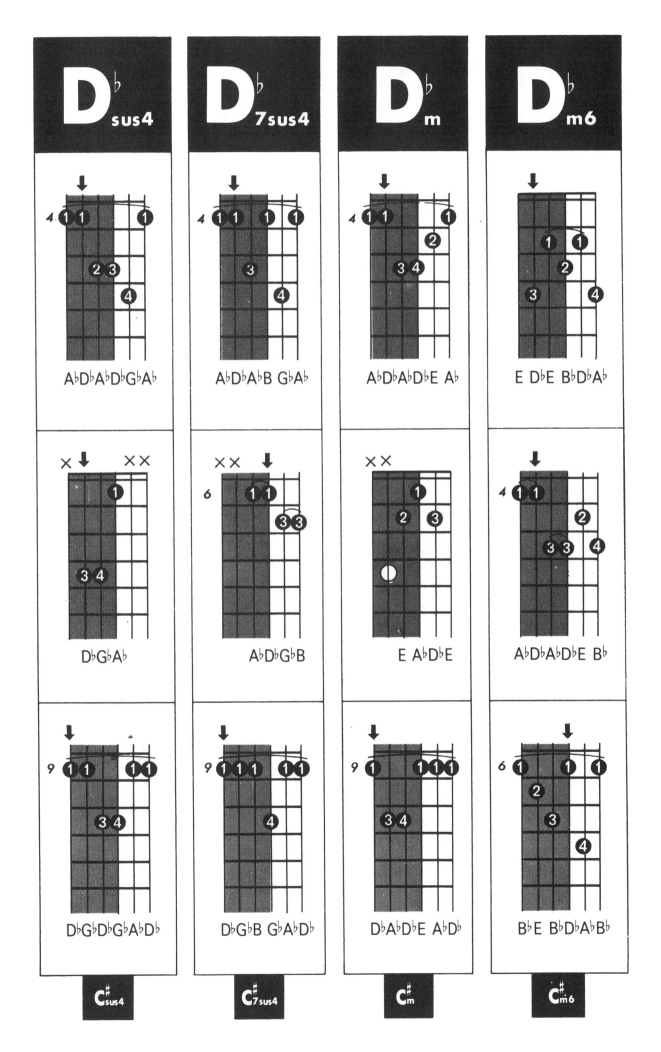

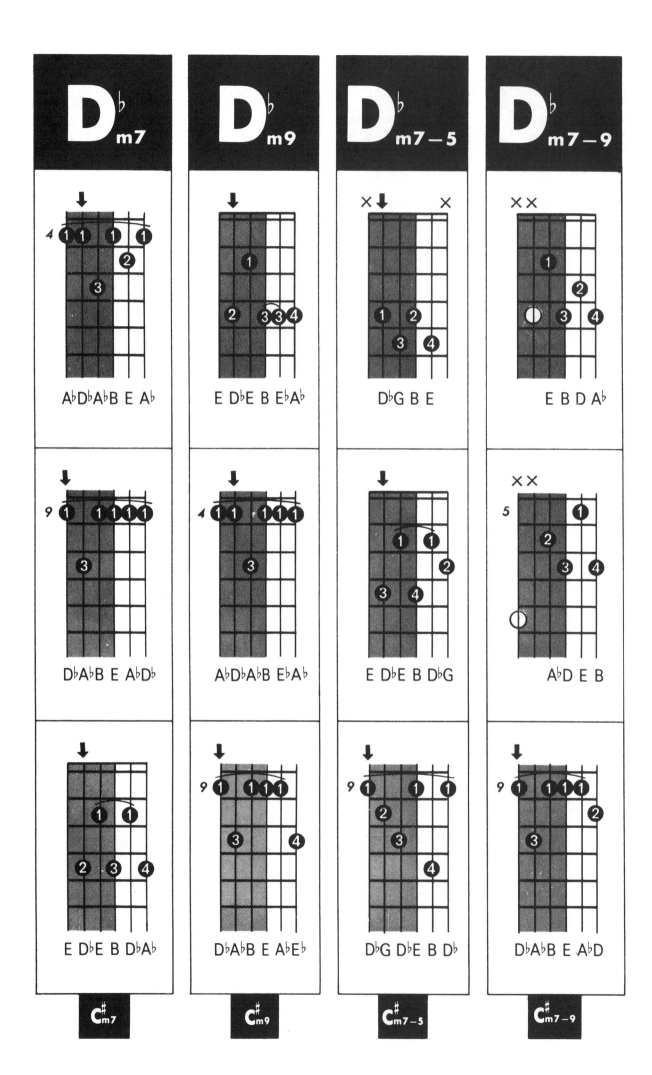

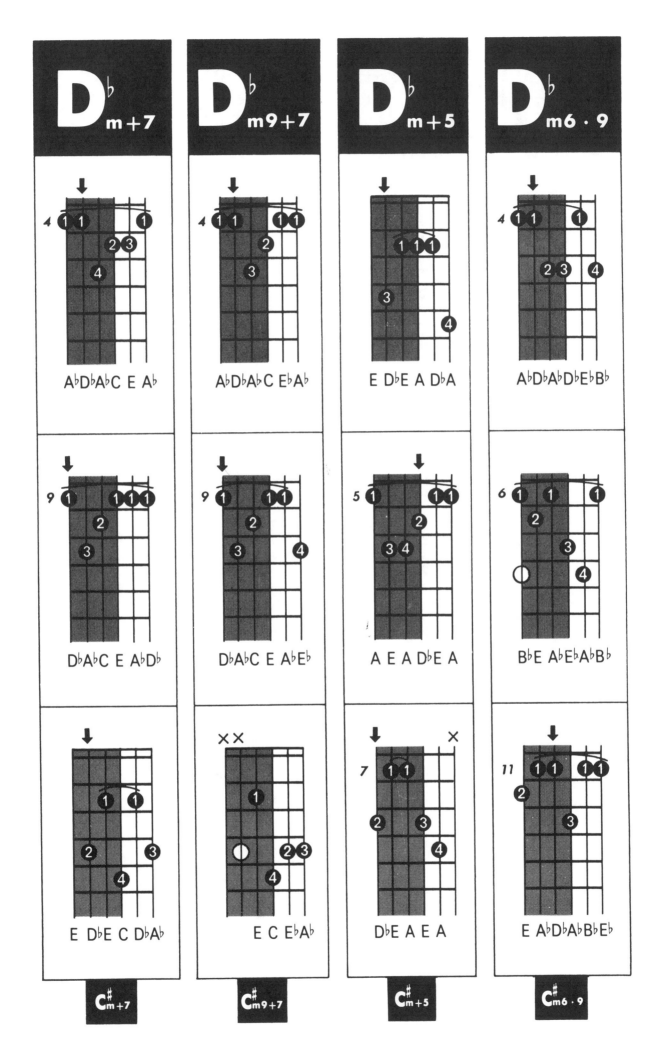

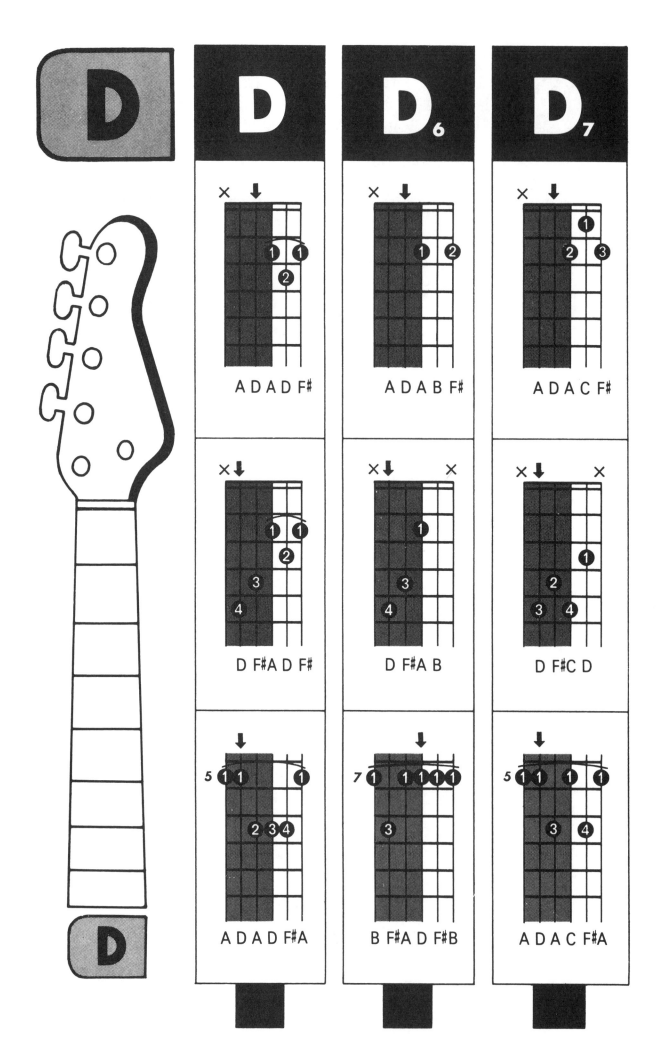

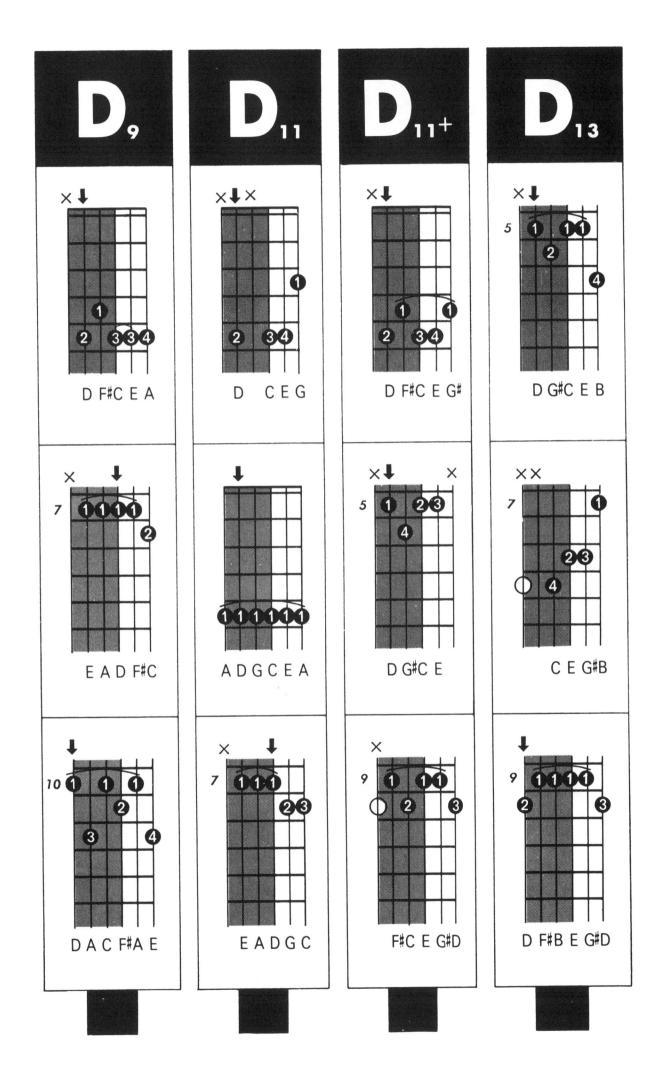

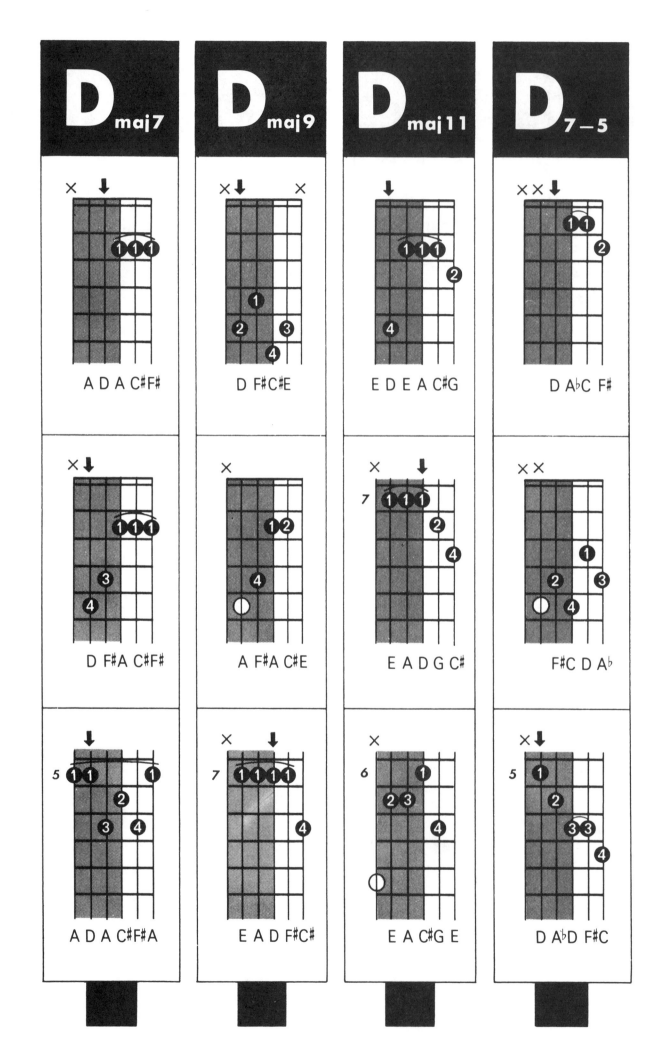

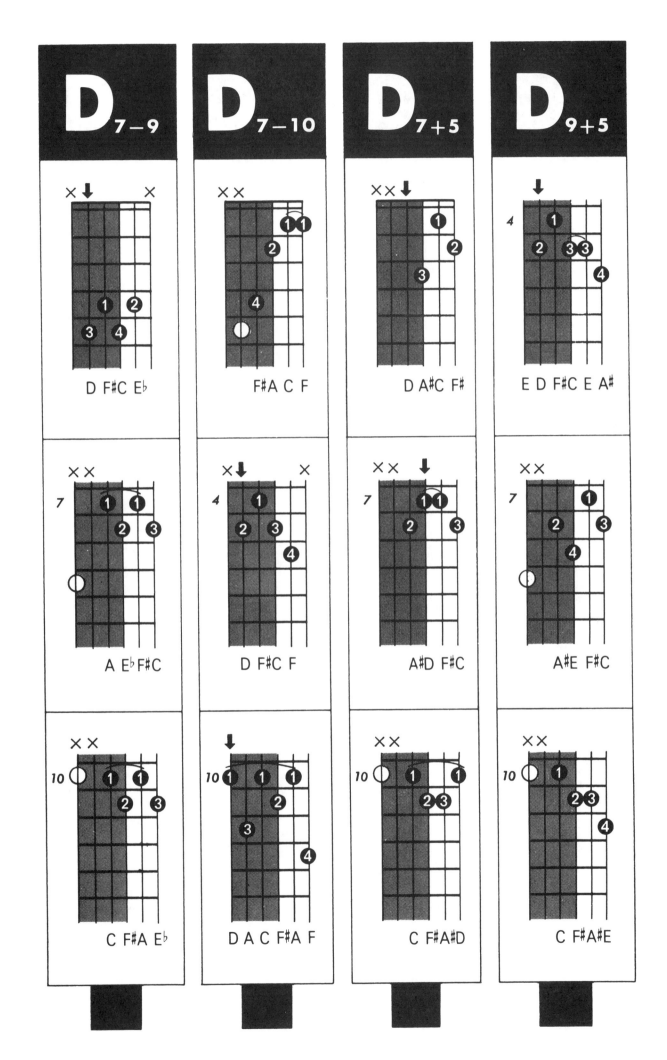

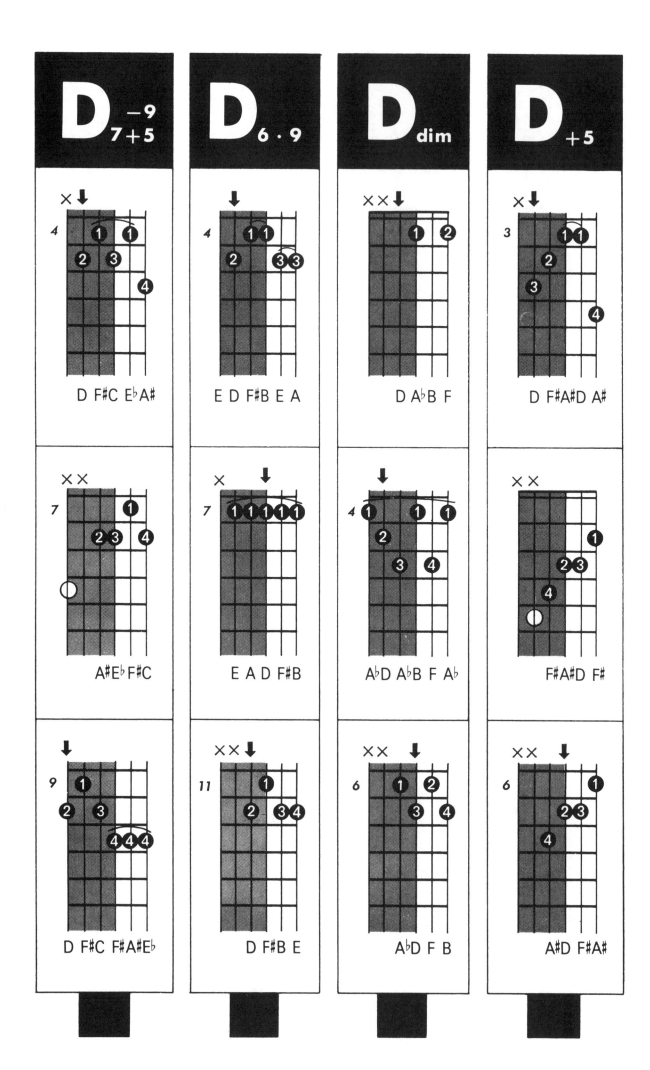

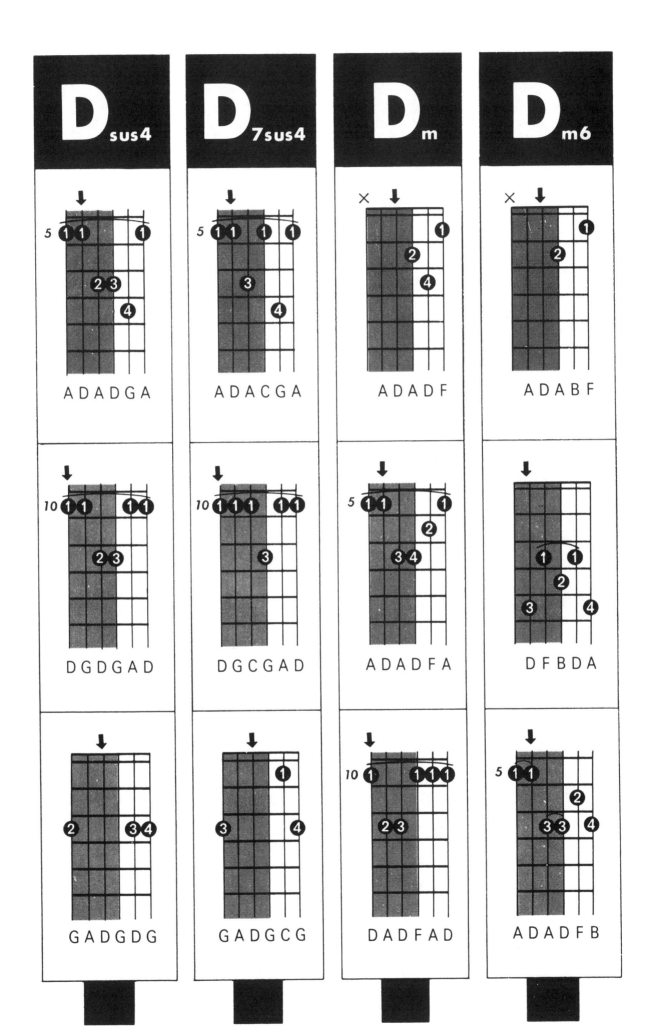

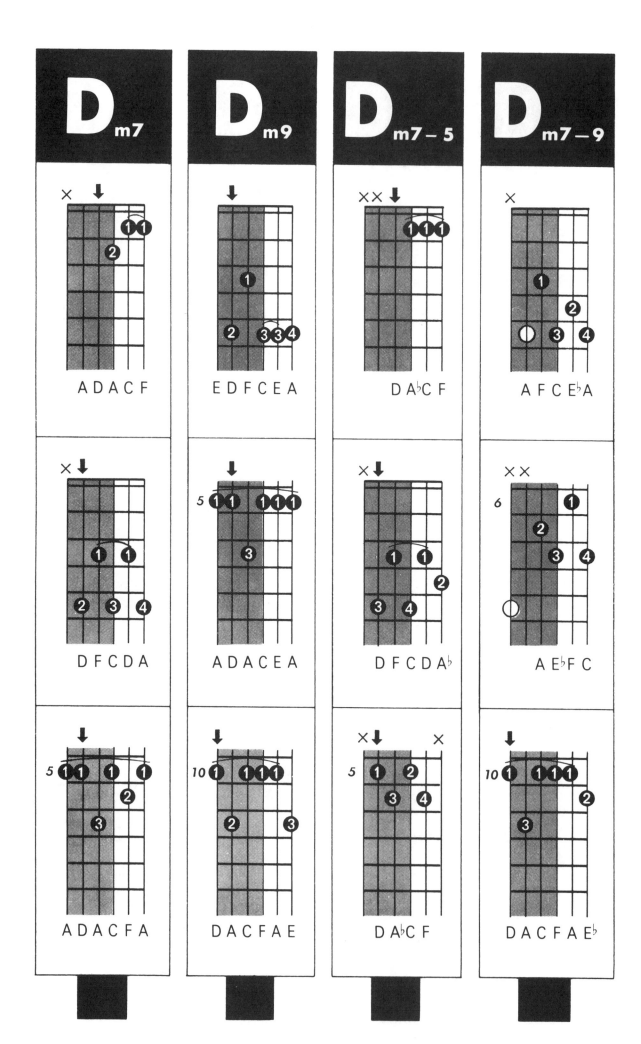

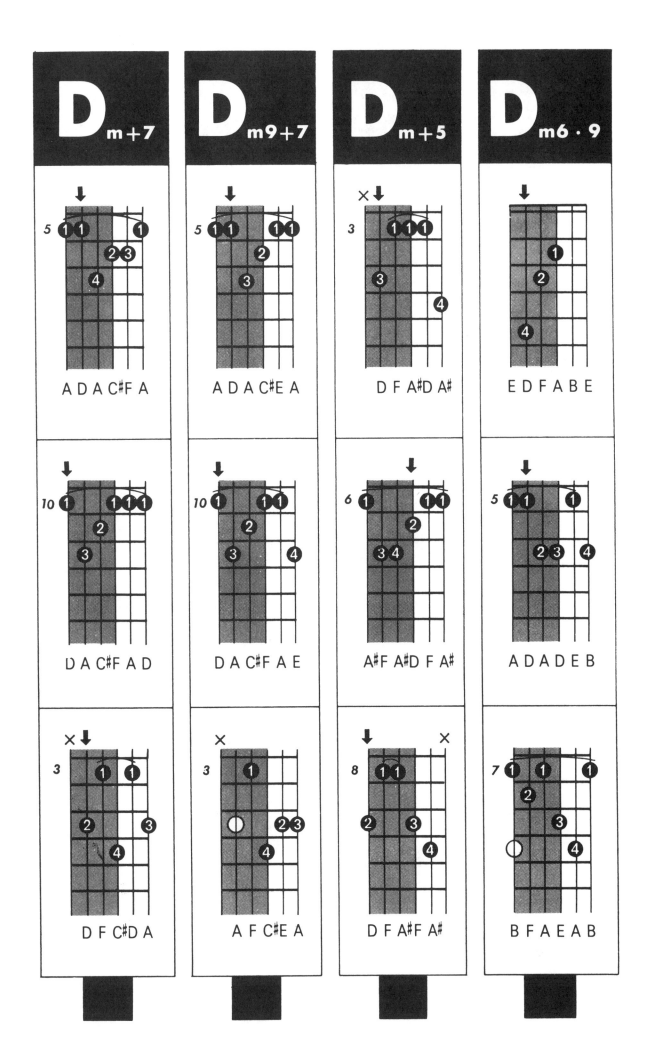

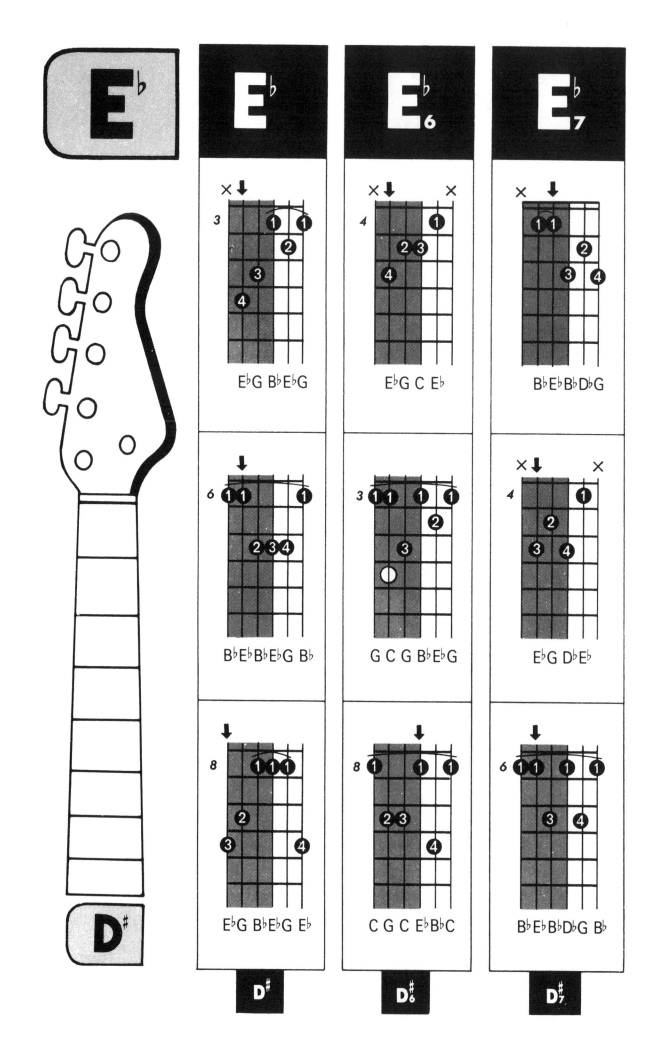

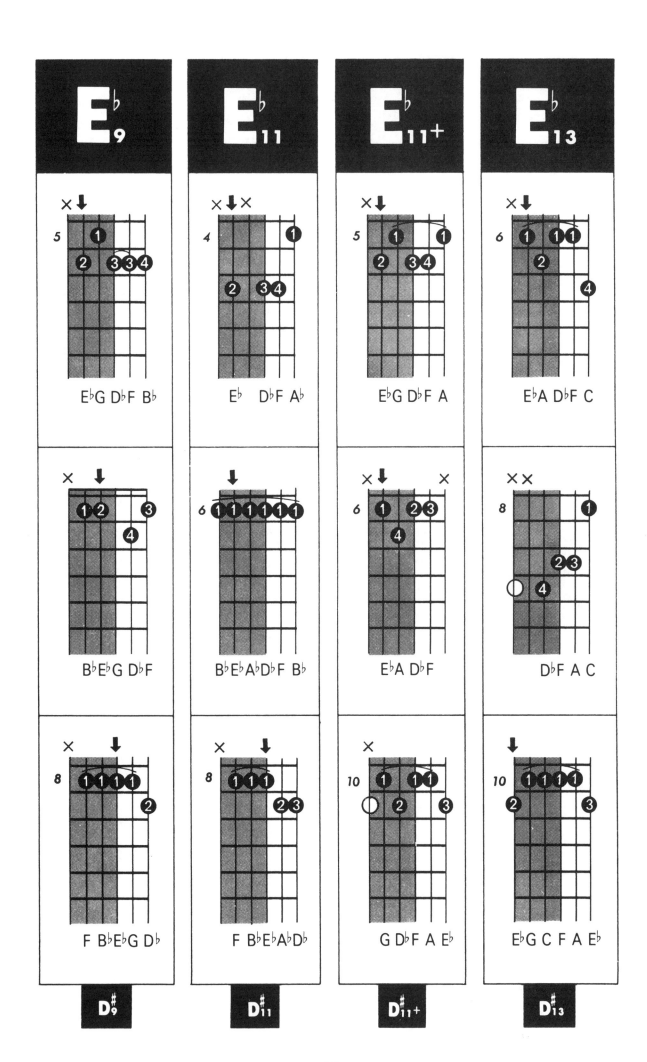

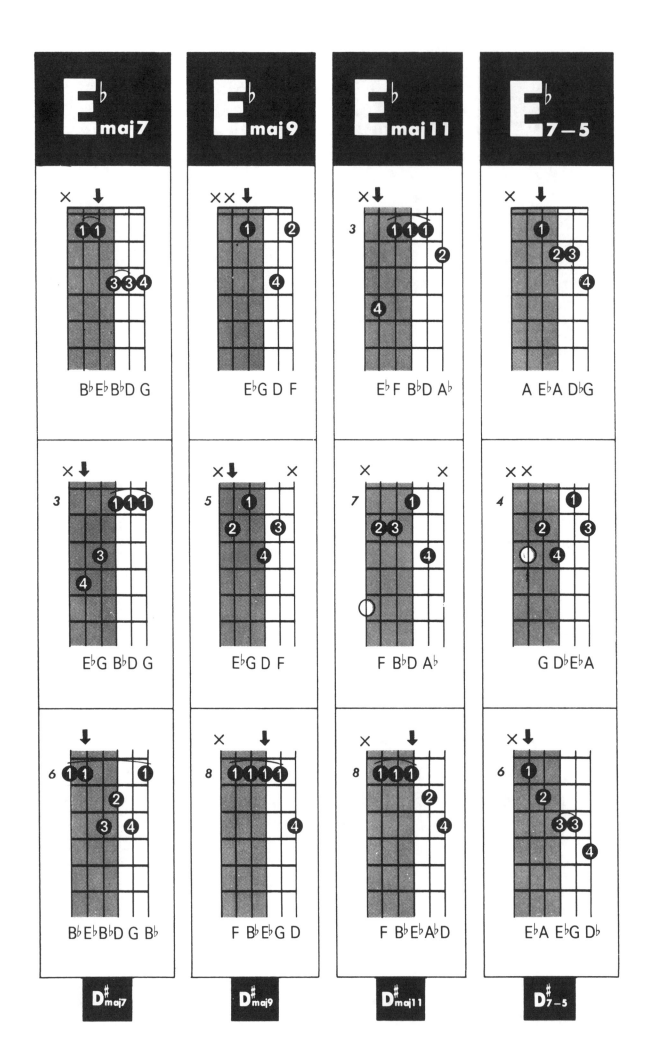

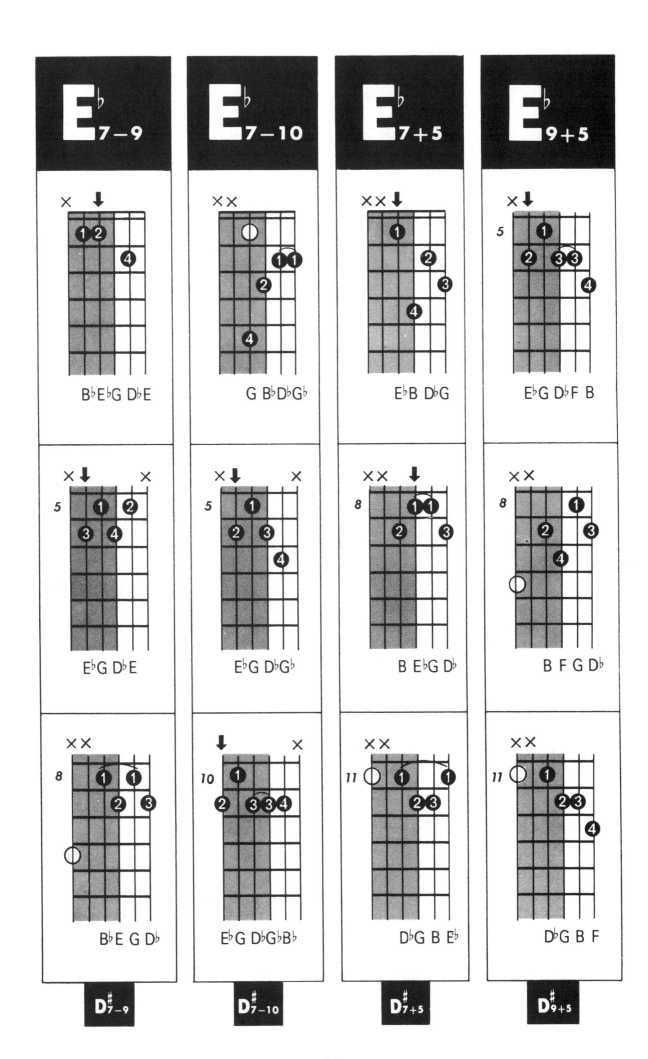

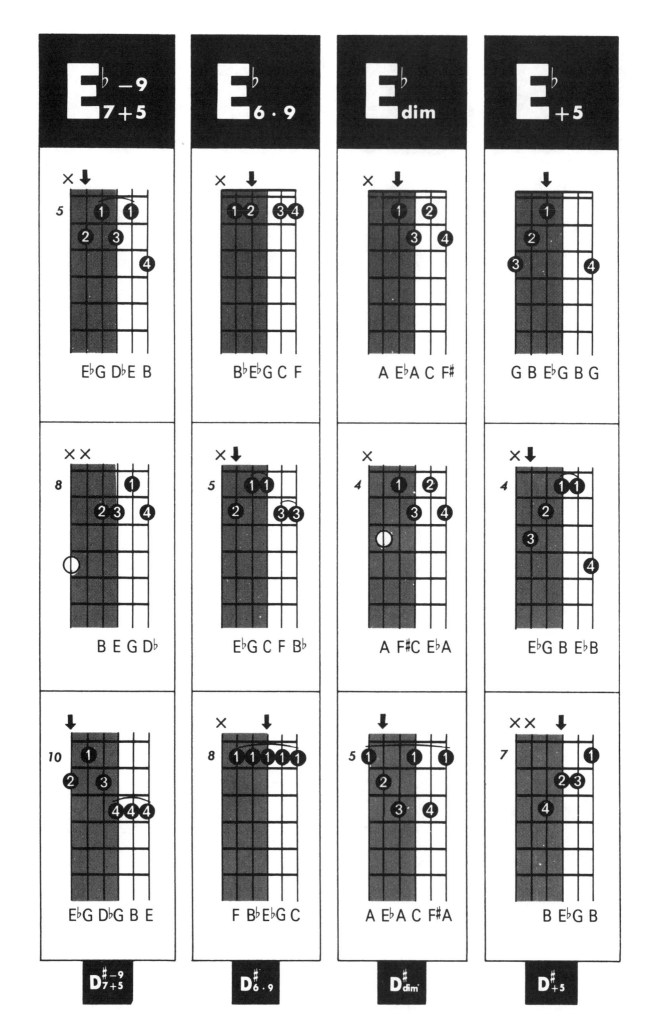

D#

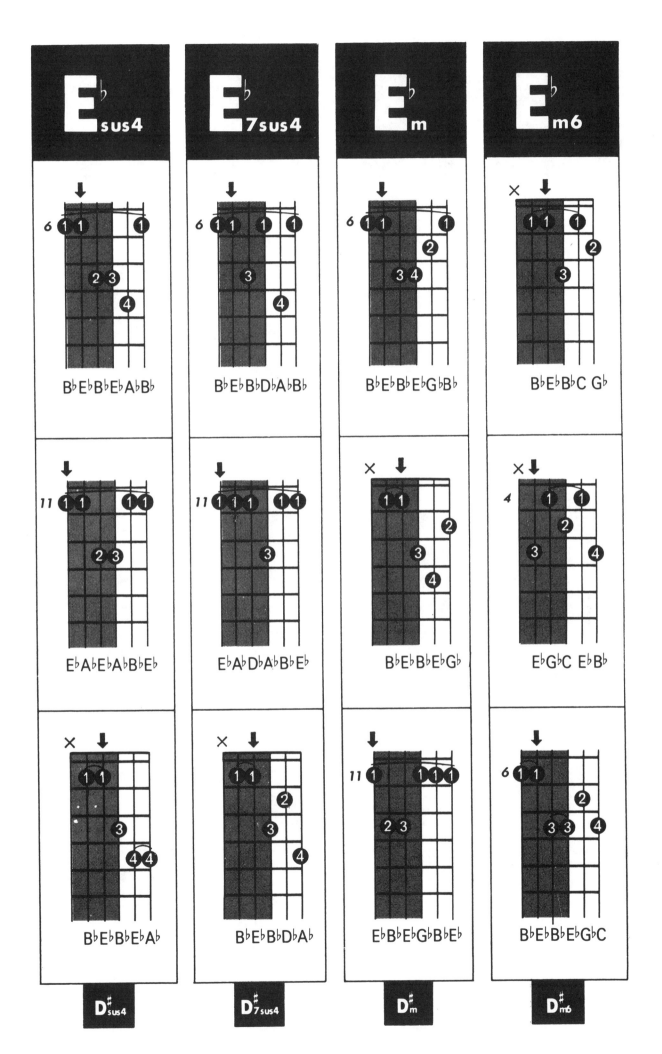

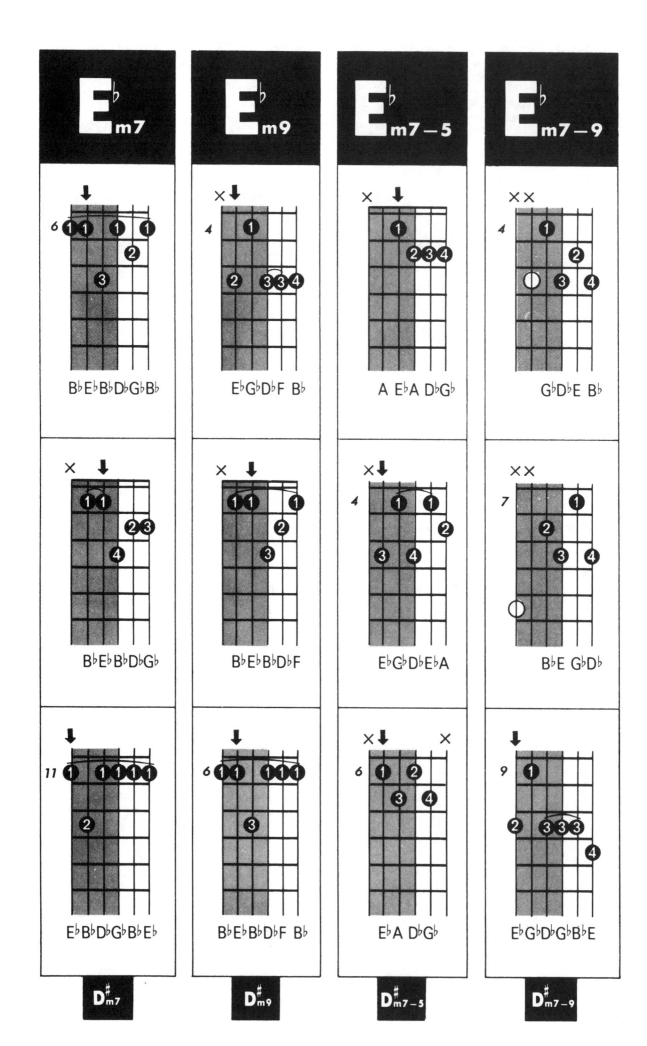

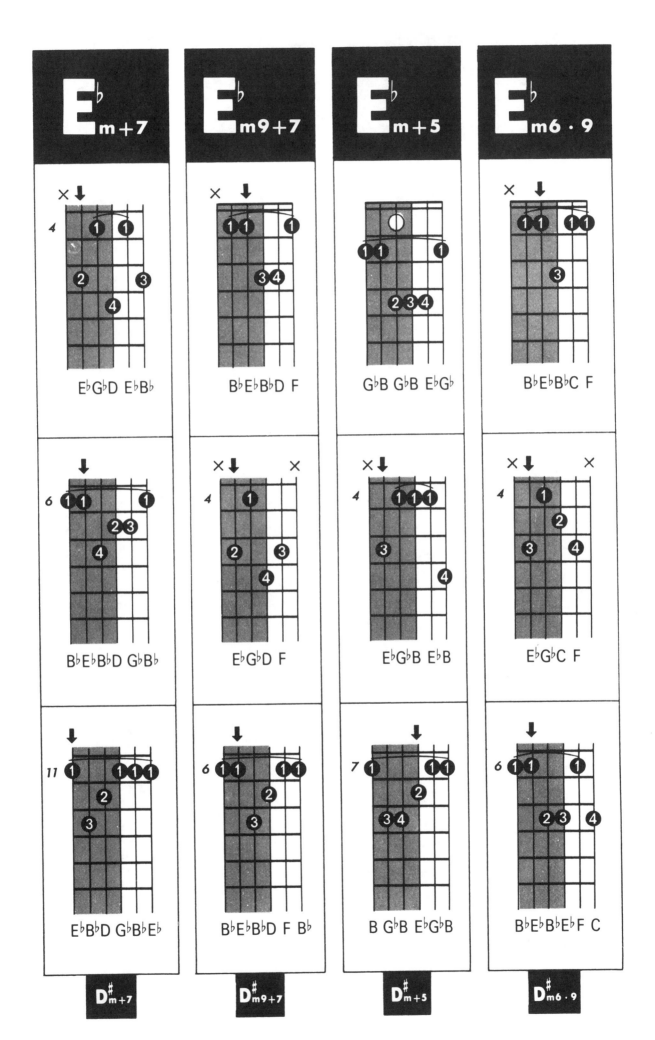

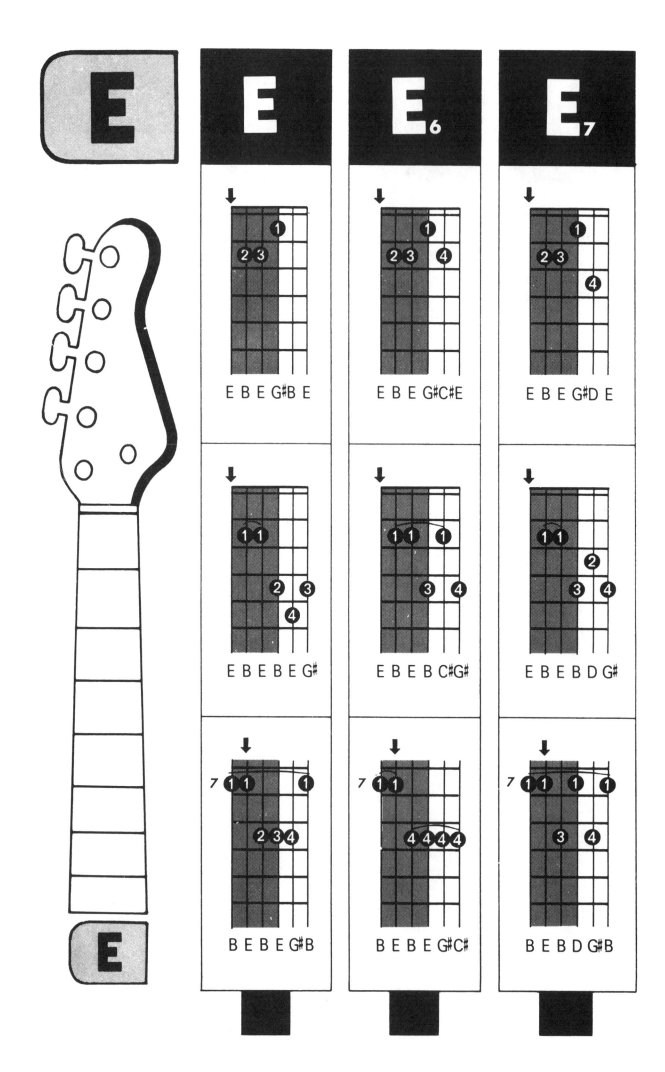

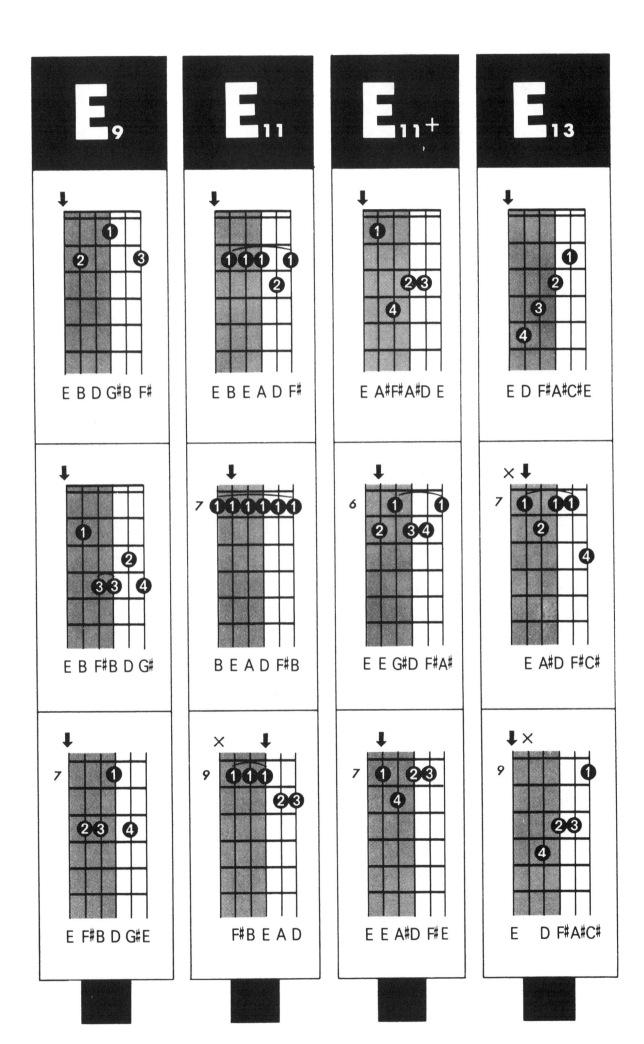

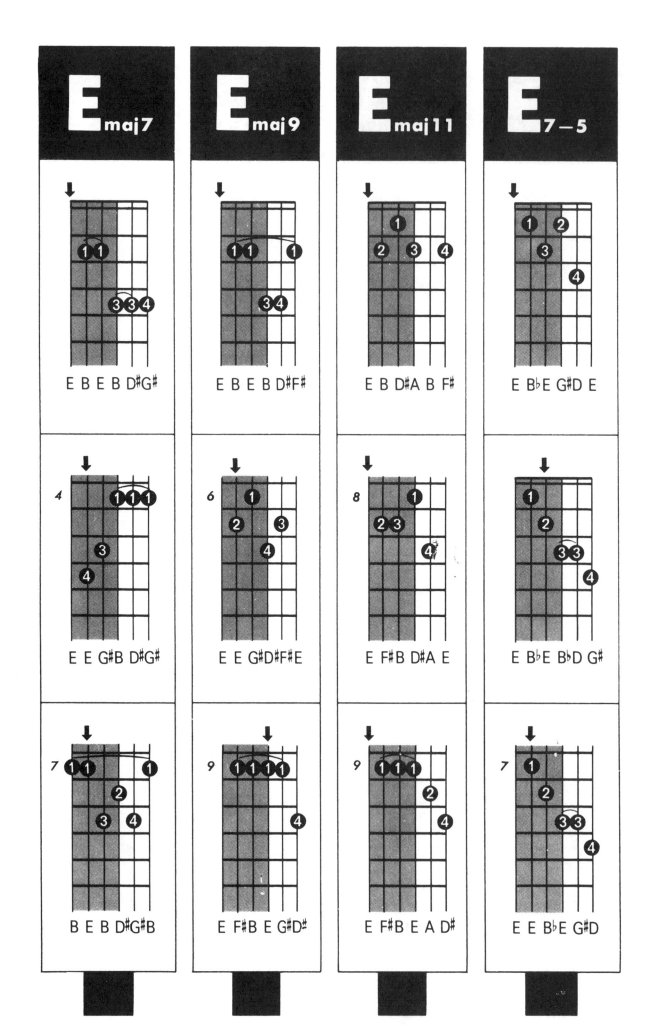

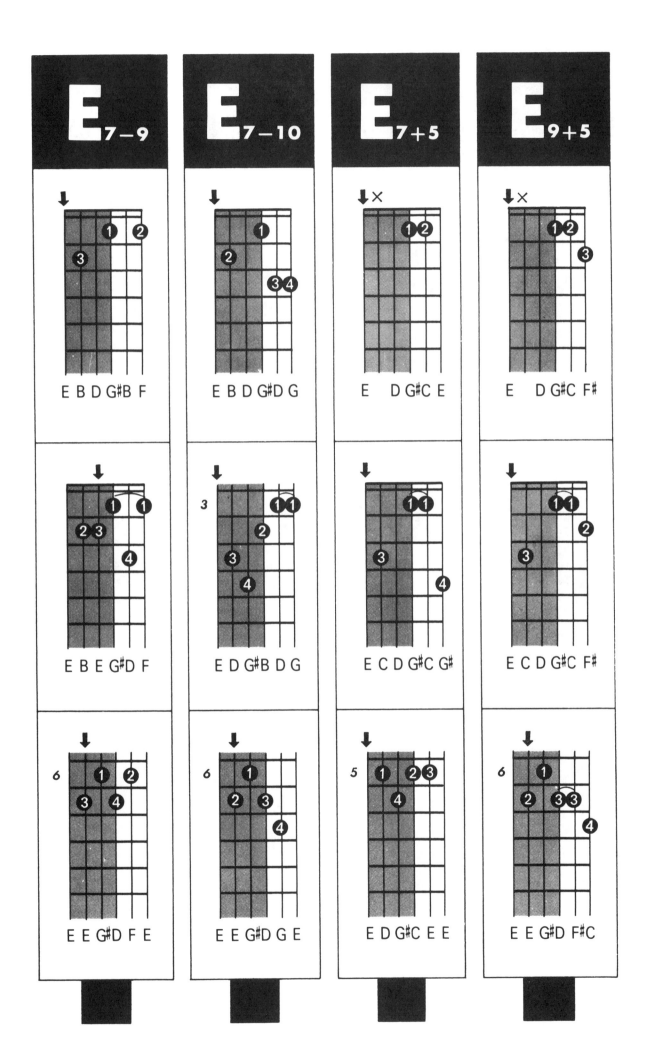

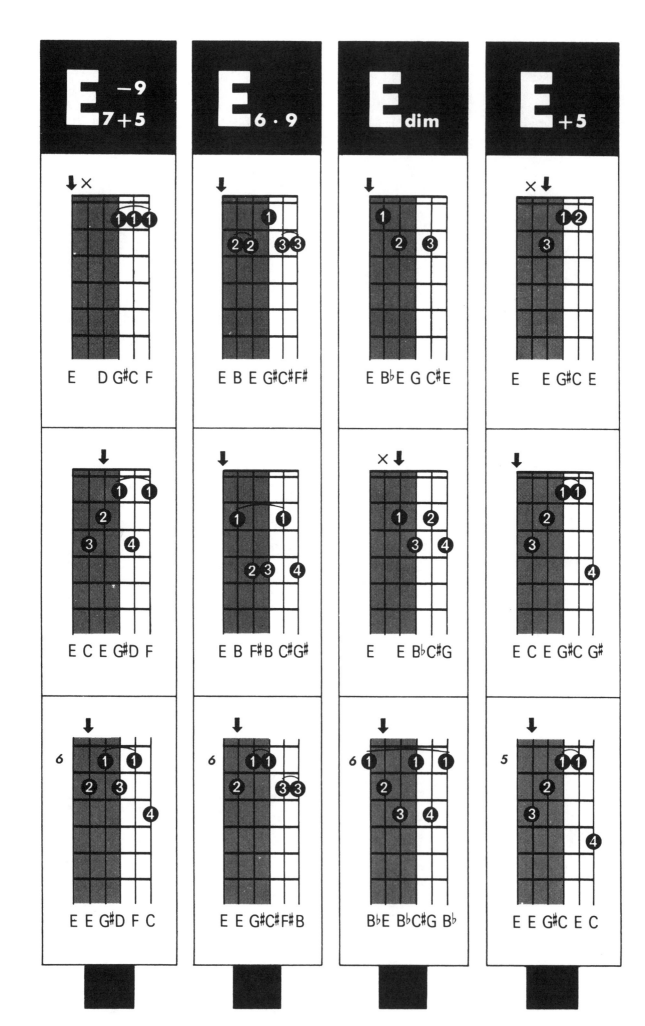

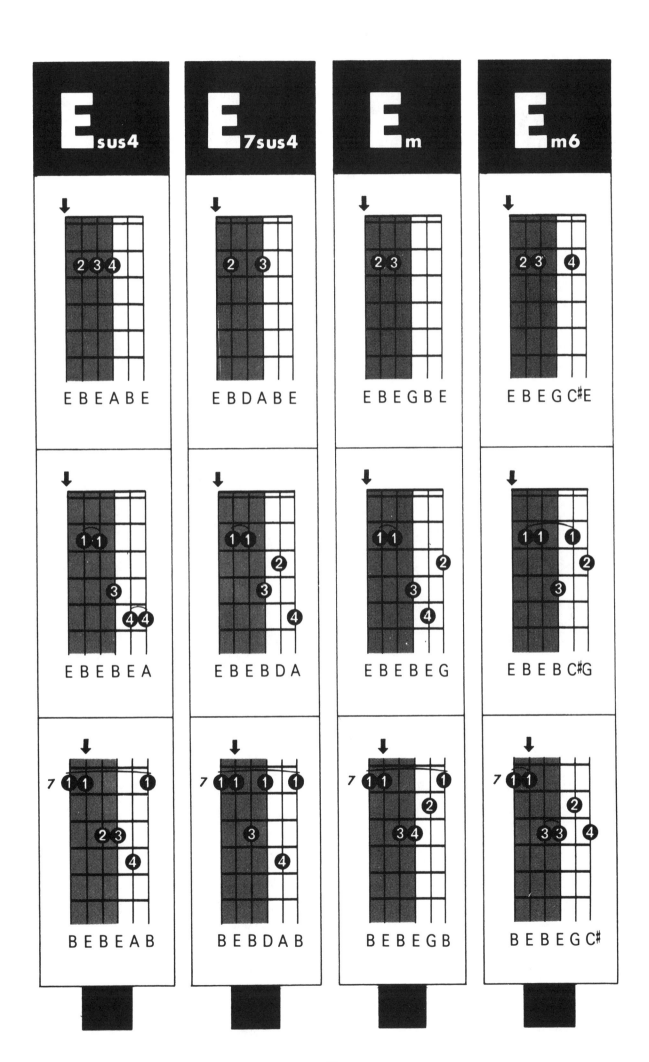

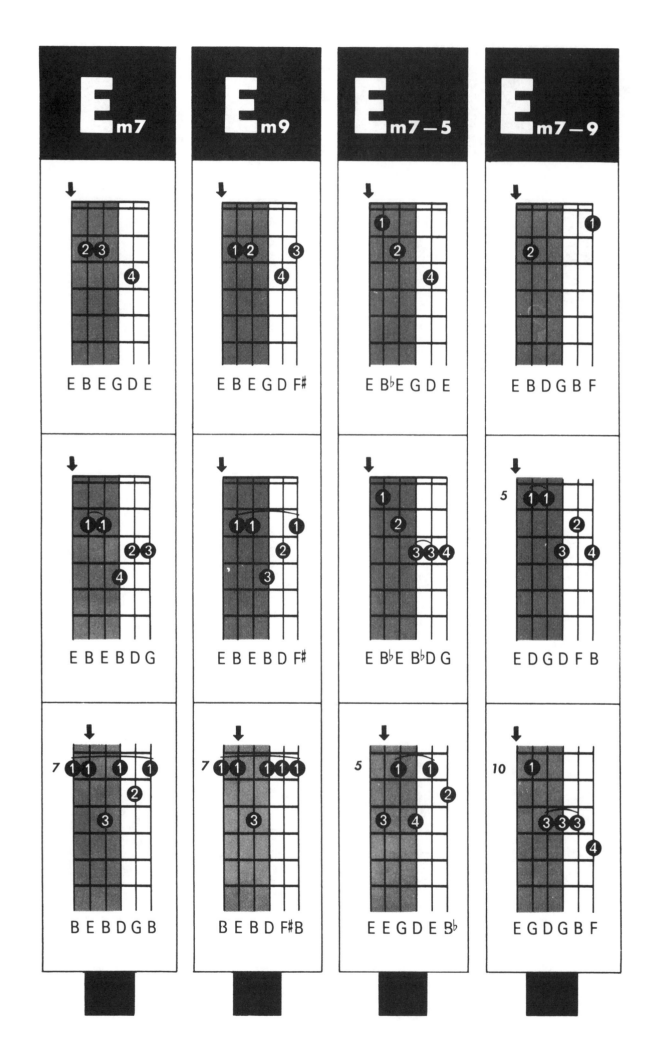

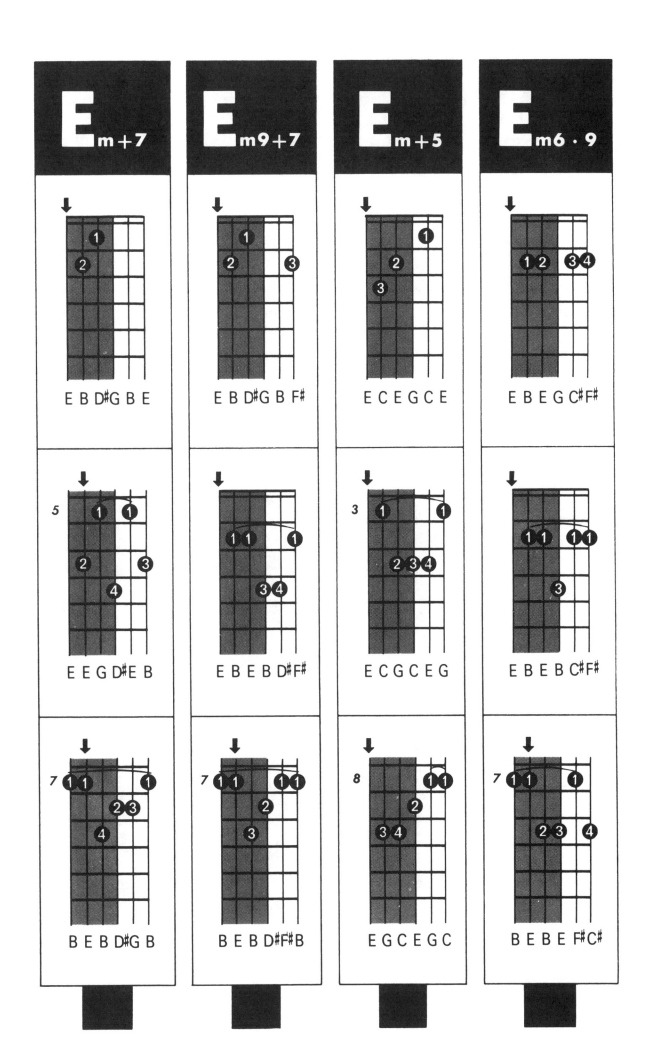

E m+7 · E m9+7 · E m+5 · E m6·9

E m+7

E B D#G B E

E E G D#E B

B E B D#G B

E m9+7

E B D#G B F#

E B E B D#F#

B E B D#F#B

E m+5

E C E G C E

E C G C E G

E G C E G C

E m6·9

E B E G C#F#

E B E B C#F#

B E B E F#C#

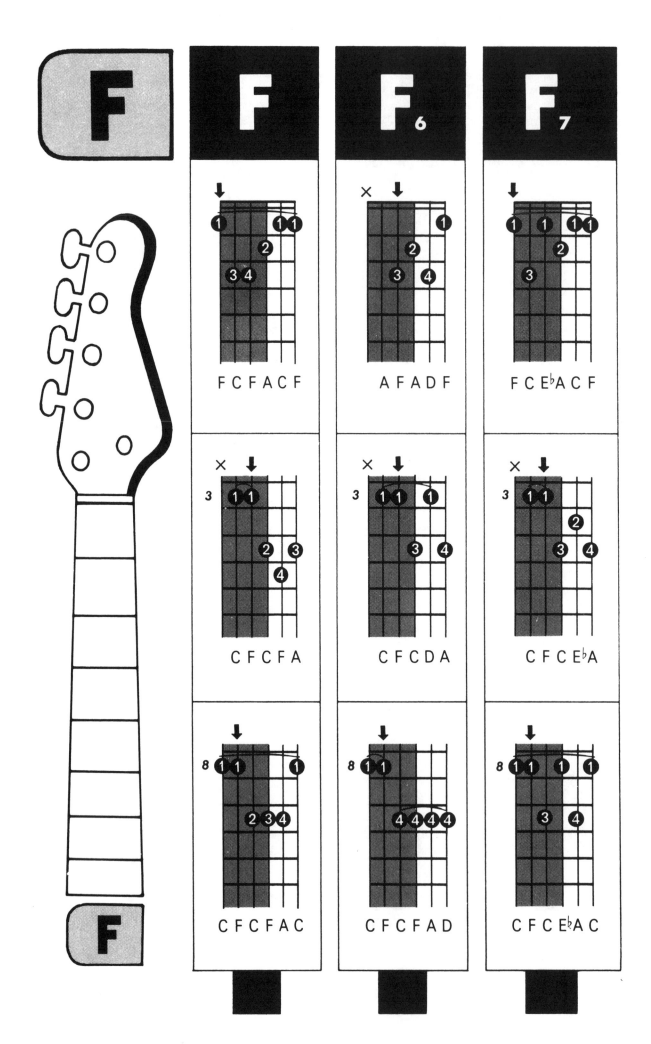

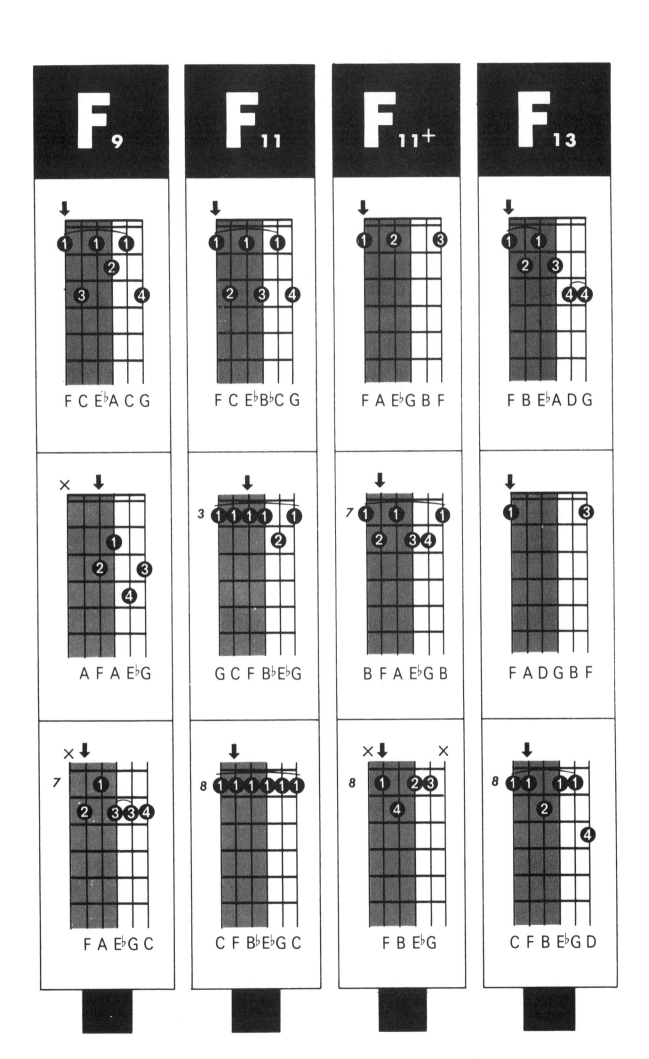

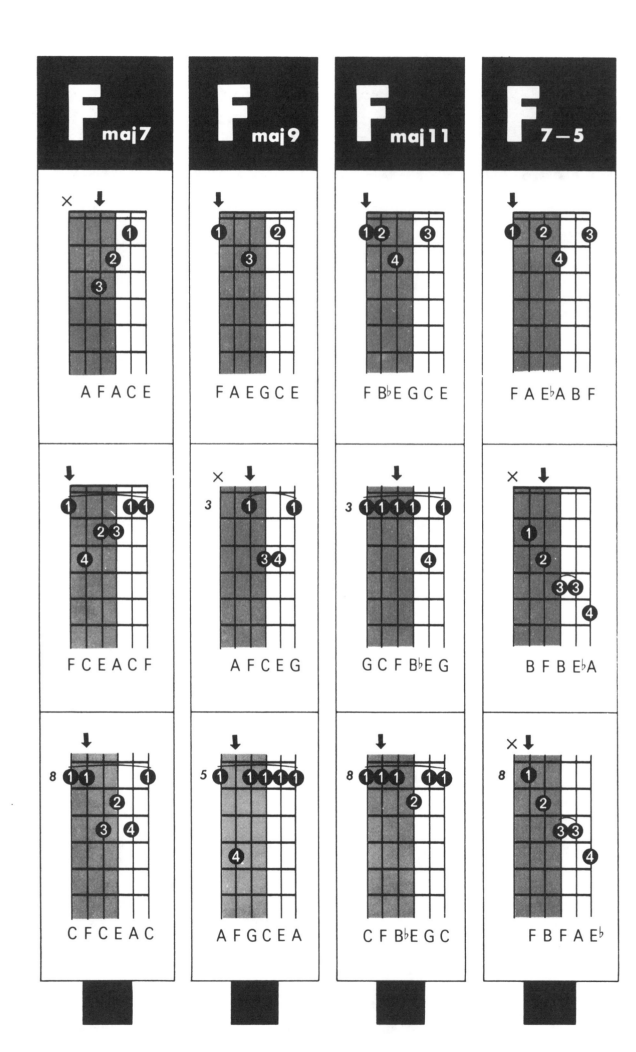

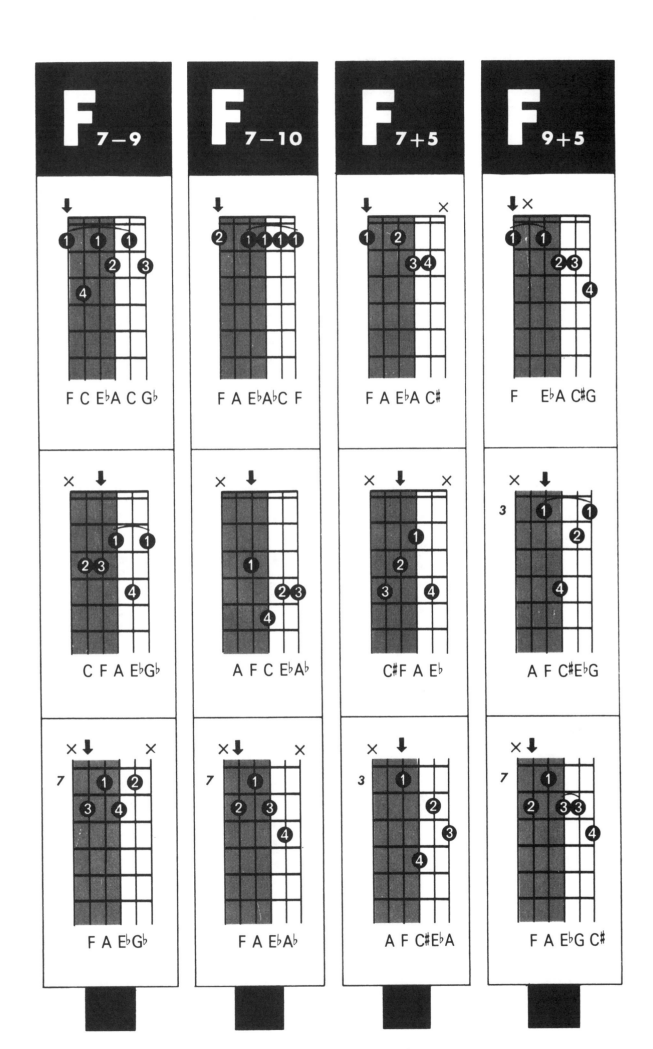

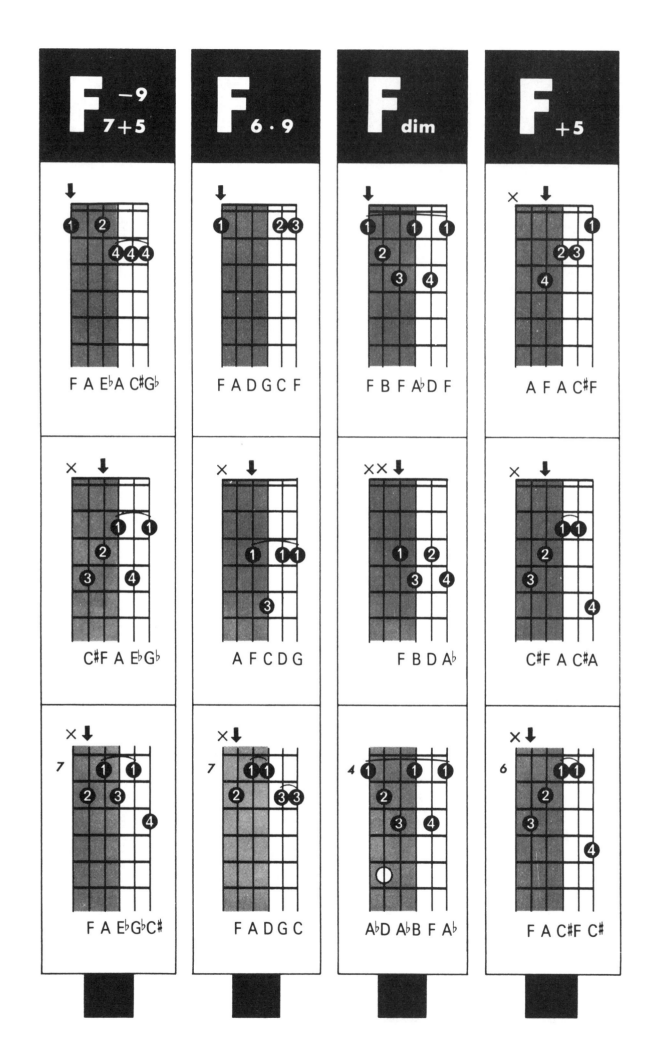

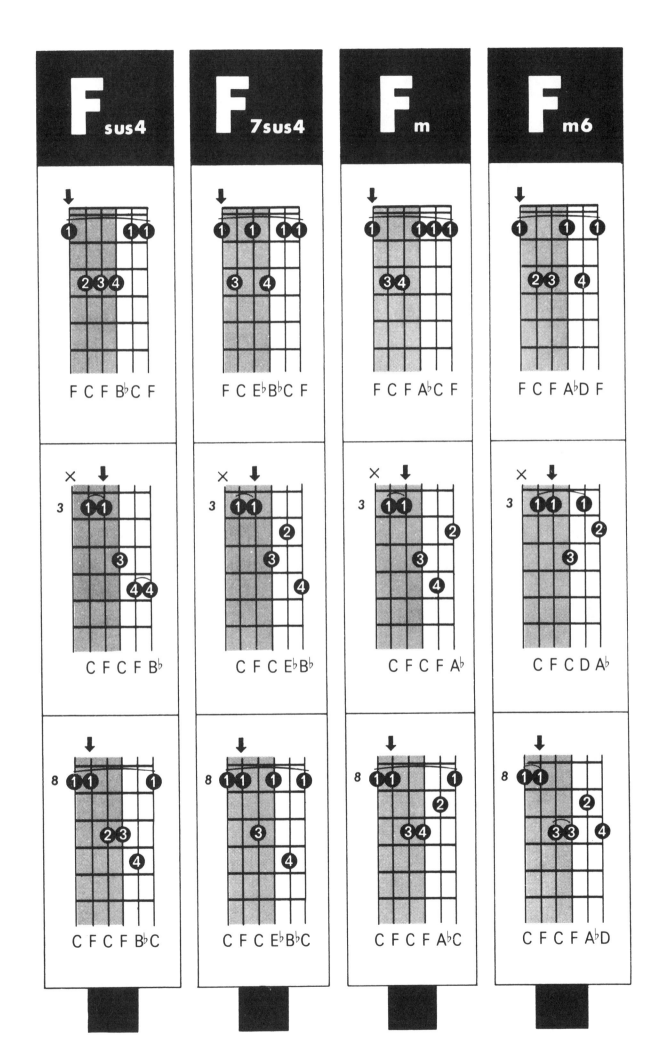

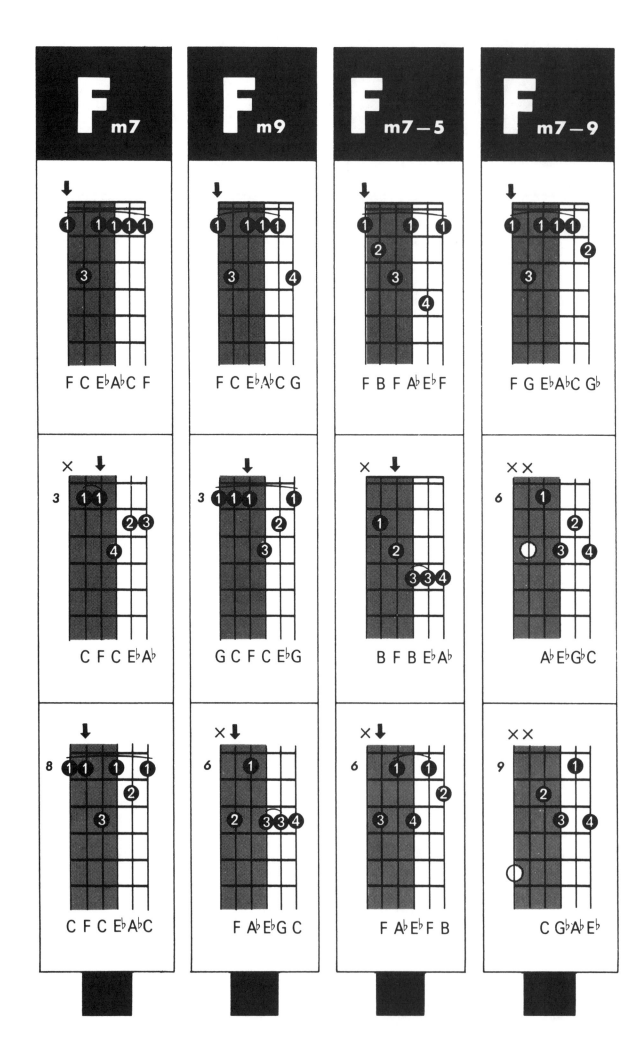

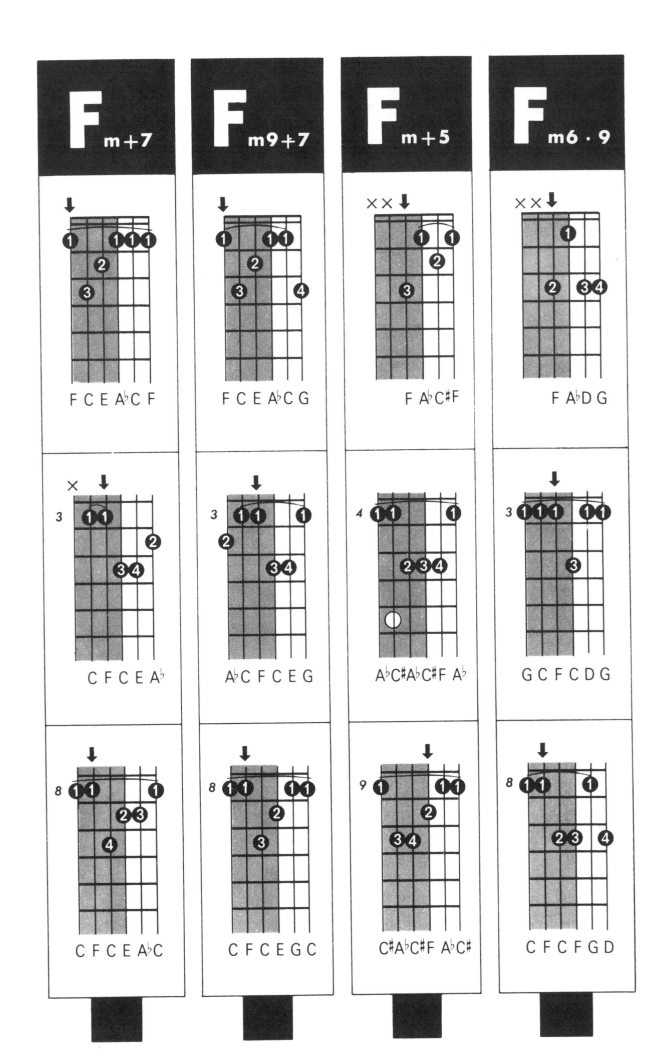

F m+7   F m9+7   F m+5   F m6·9

F C E A♭ C F   F C E A♭ C G   F A♭ C♯ F   F A♭ D G

C F C E A♭   A♭ C F C E G   A♭ C♯ A♭ C♯ F A♭   G C F C D G

C F C E A♭ C   C F C E G C   C♯ A♭ C♯ F A♭ C♯   C F C F G D

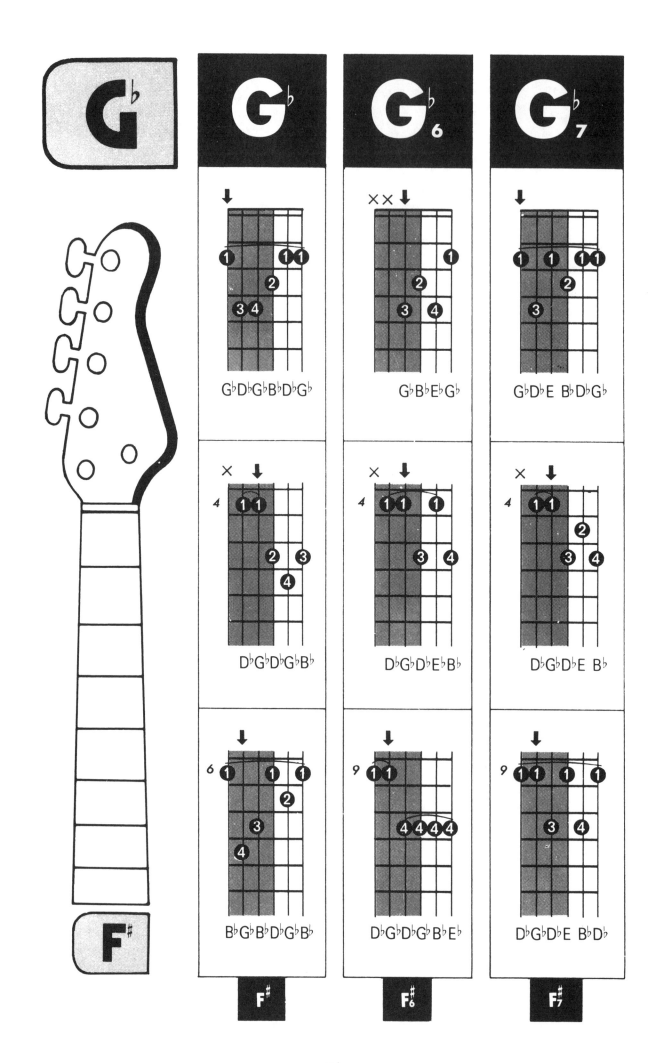

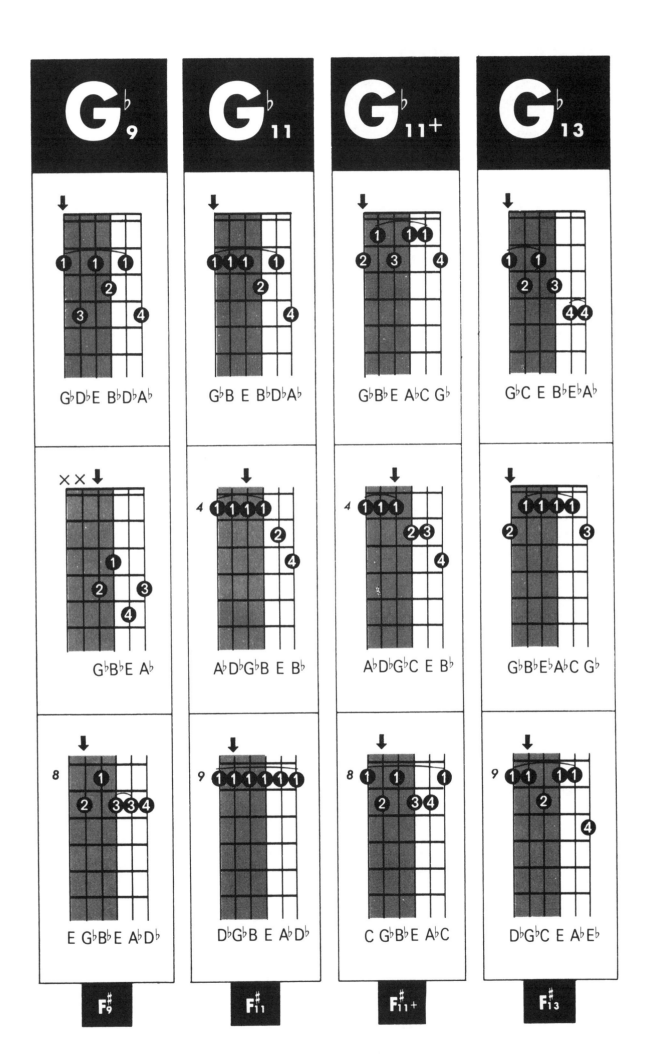

57

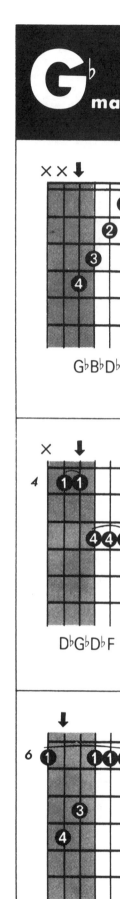

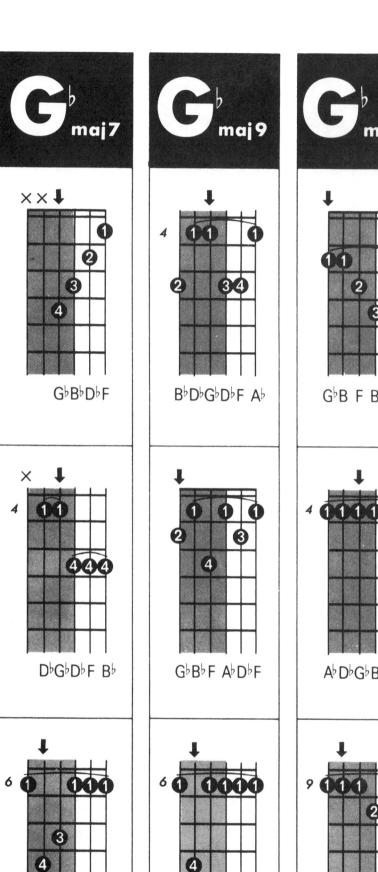

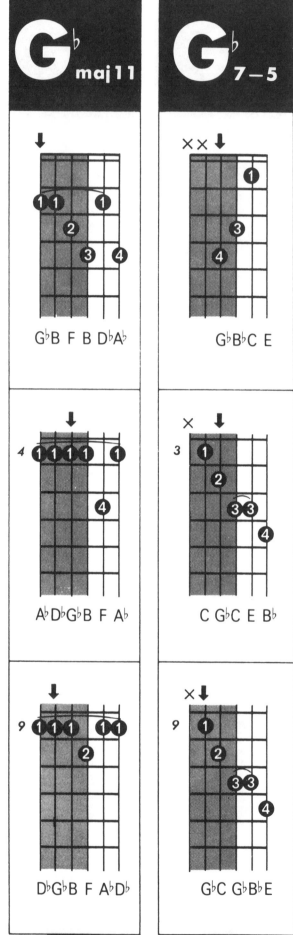

G♭maj7

G♭B♭D♭F

D♭G♭D♭F B♭

B♭G♭B♭D♭F B♭

F#maj7

G♭maj9

B♭D♭G♭D♭F A♭

G♭B♭F A♭D♭F

B♭G♭A♭D♭F B♭

F#maj9

G♭maj11

G♭B F B D♭A♭

A♭D♭G♭B F A♭

D♭G♭B F A♭D♭

F#maj11

G♭7−5

G♭B♭C E

C G♭C E B♭

G♭C G♭B♭E

F#7−5

58

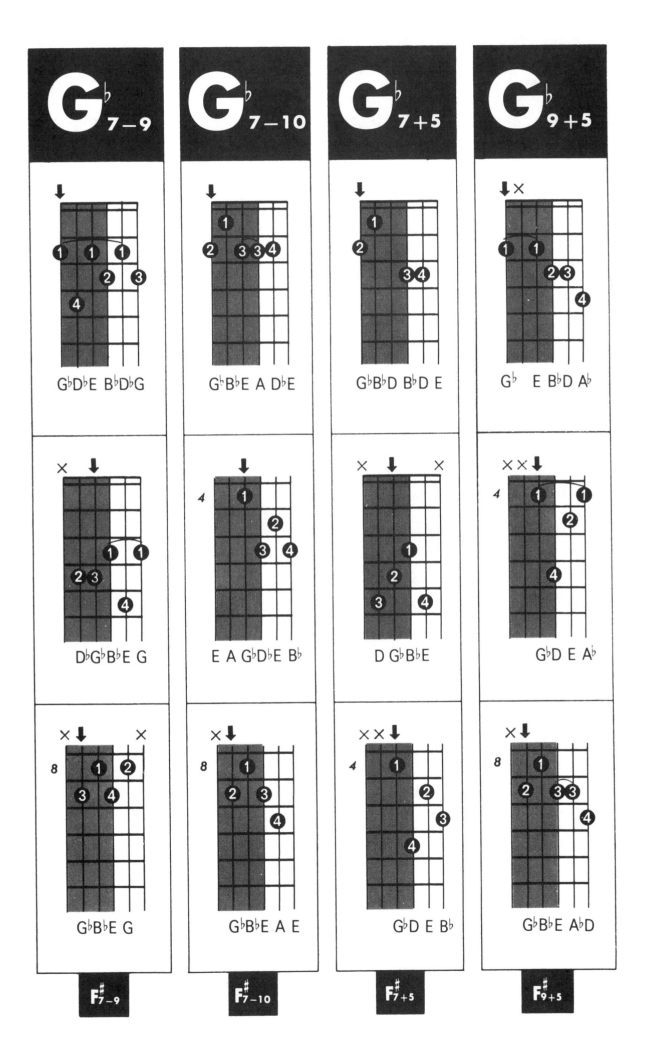

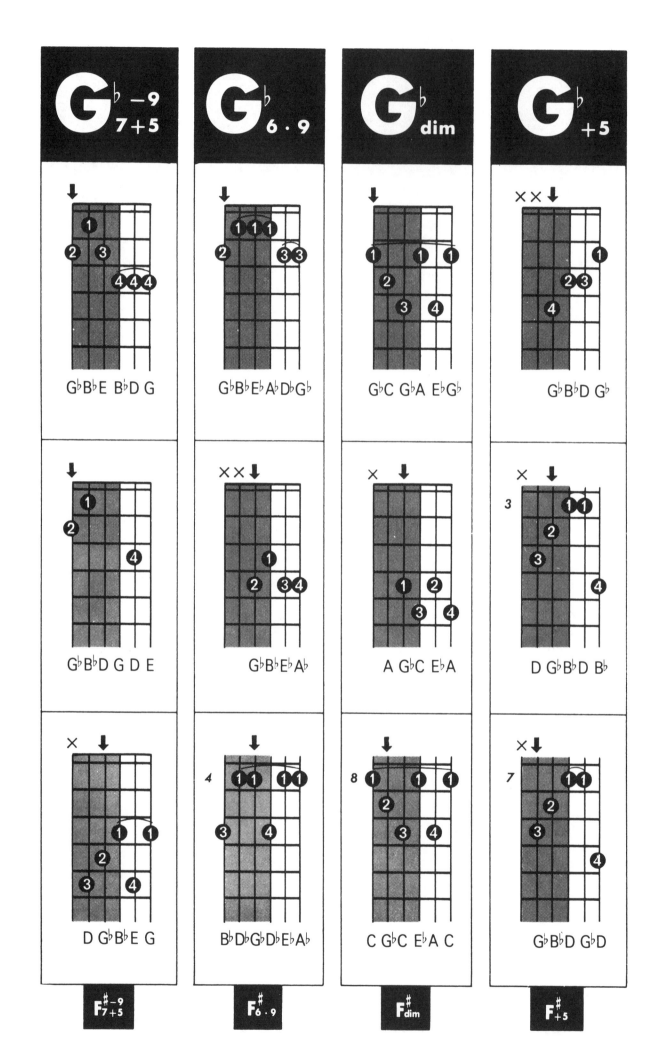

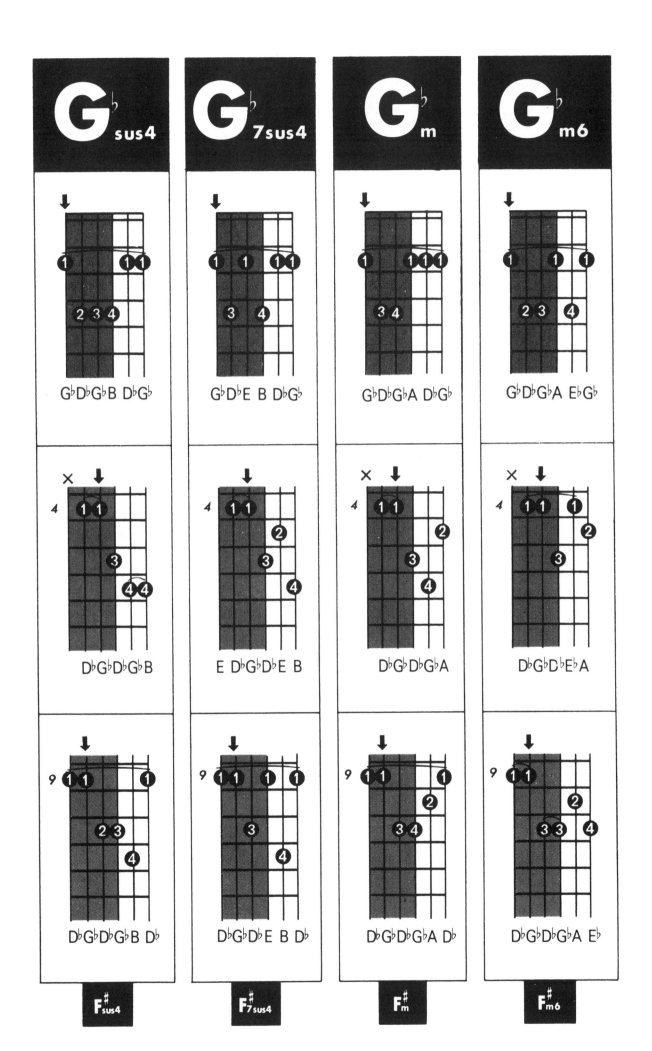

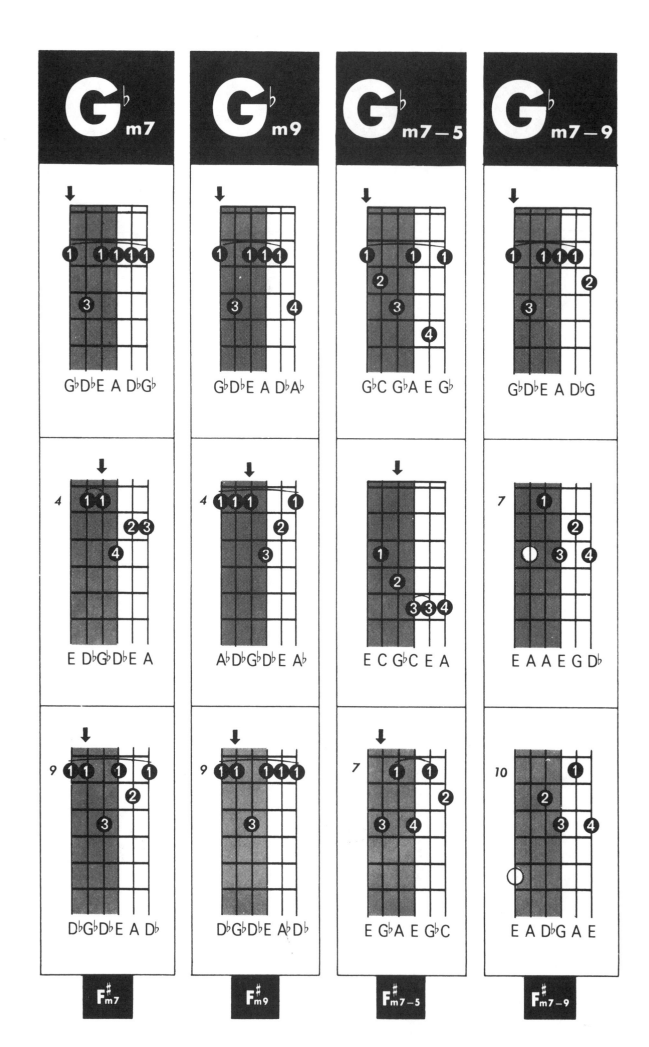

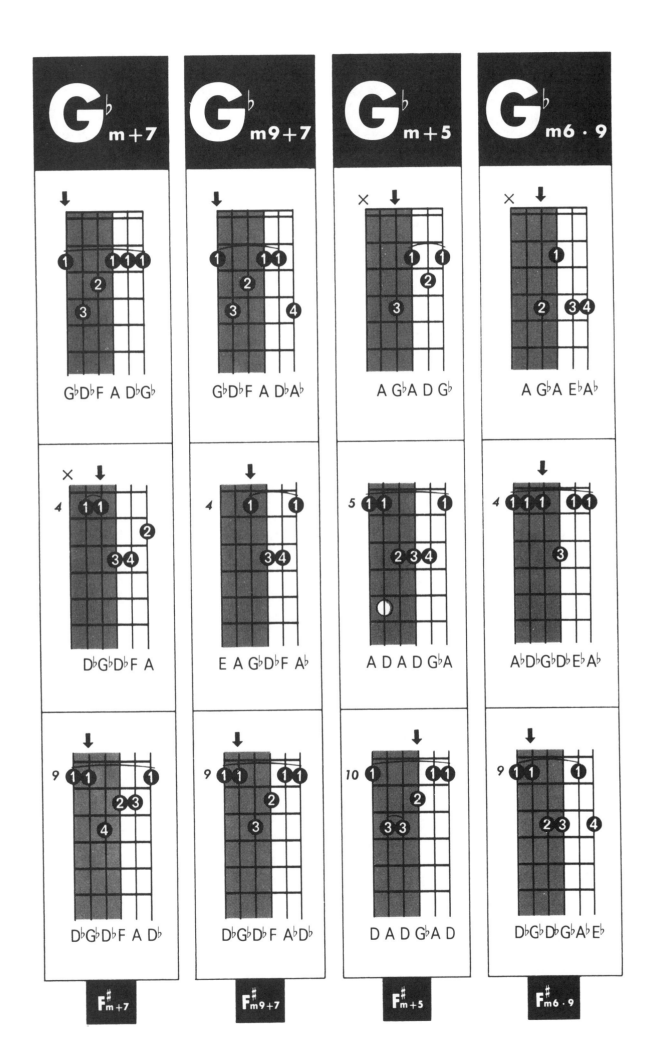

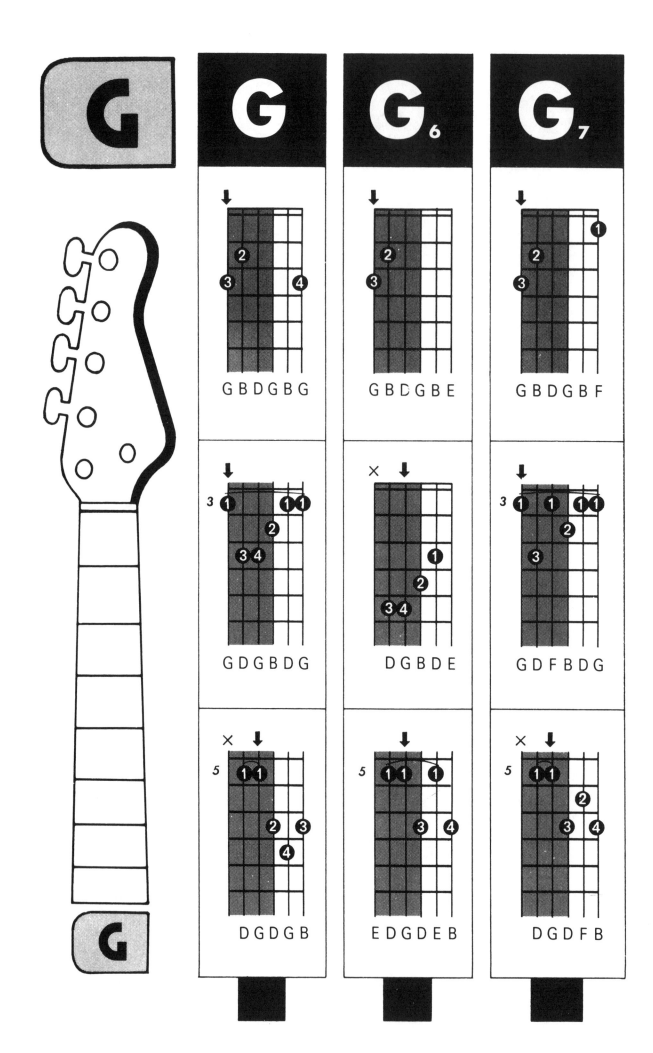

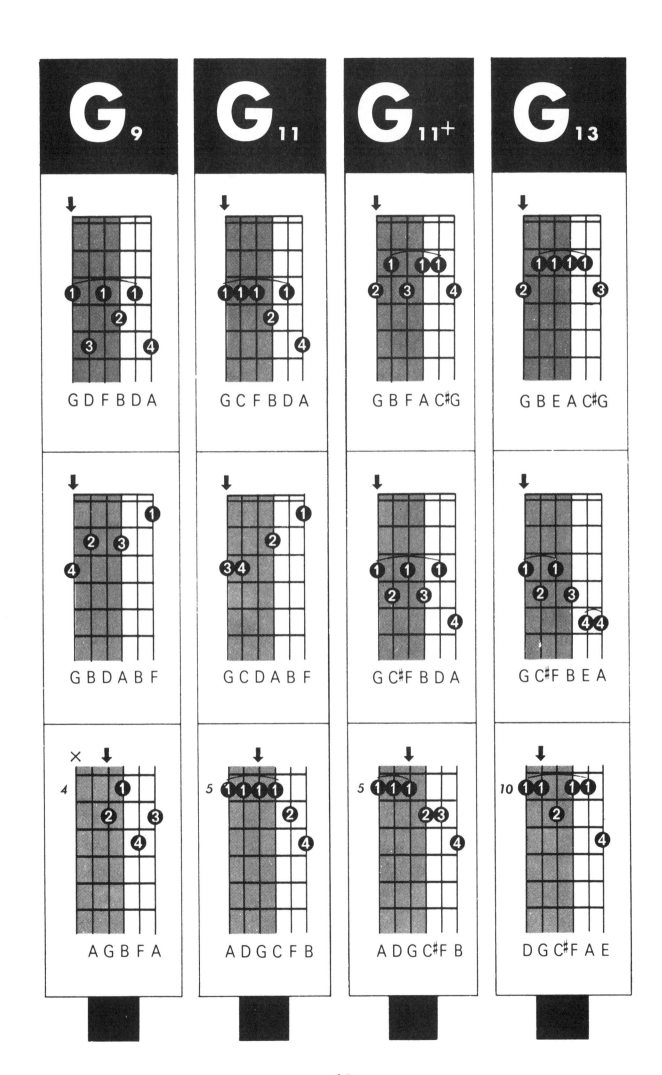

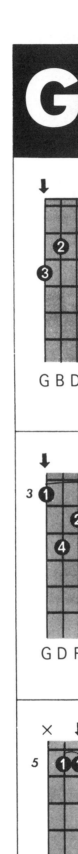

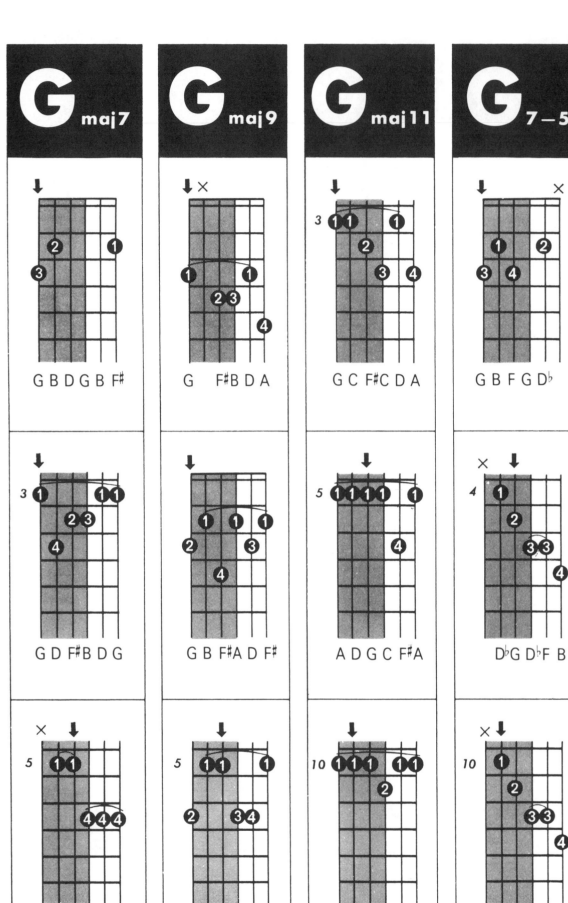

Gmaj7   Gmaj9   Gmaj11   G7−5

G B D G B F#   G F#B D A   G C F#C D A   G B F G D♭

G D F#B D G   G B F#A D F#   A D G C F#A   D♭G D♭F B

D G D F#B   B D G D F#A   D G C F#A D   G D♭G B F

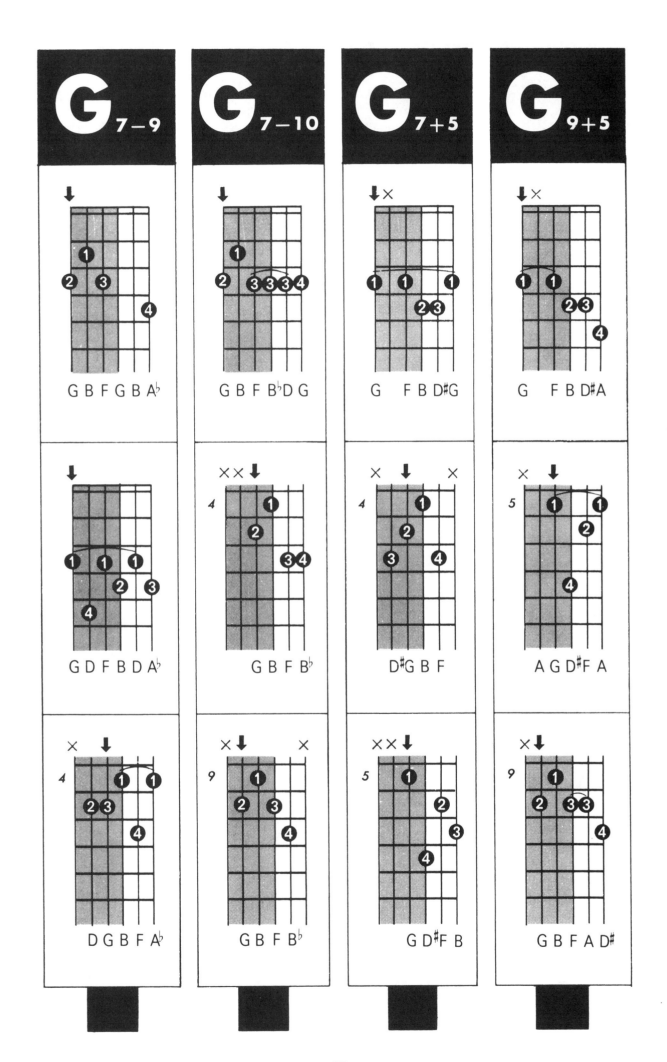

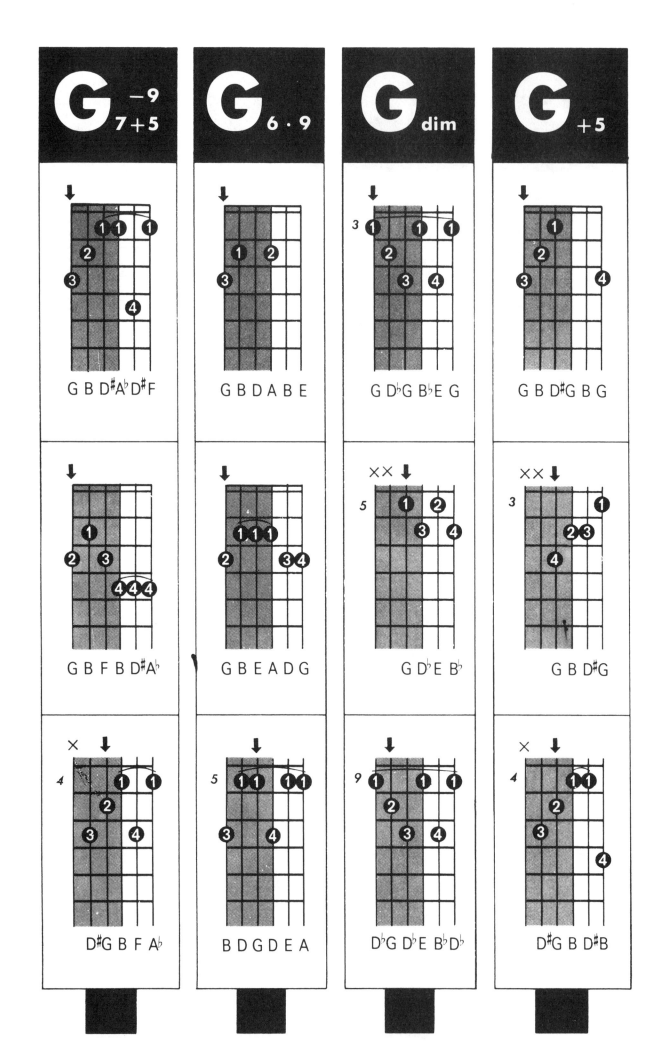

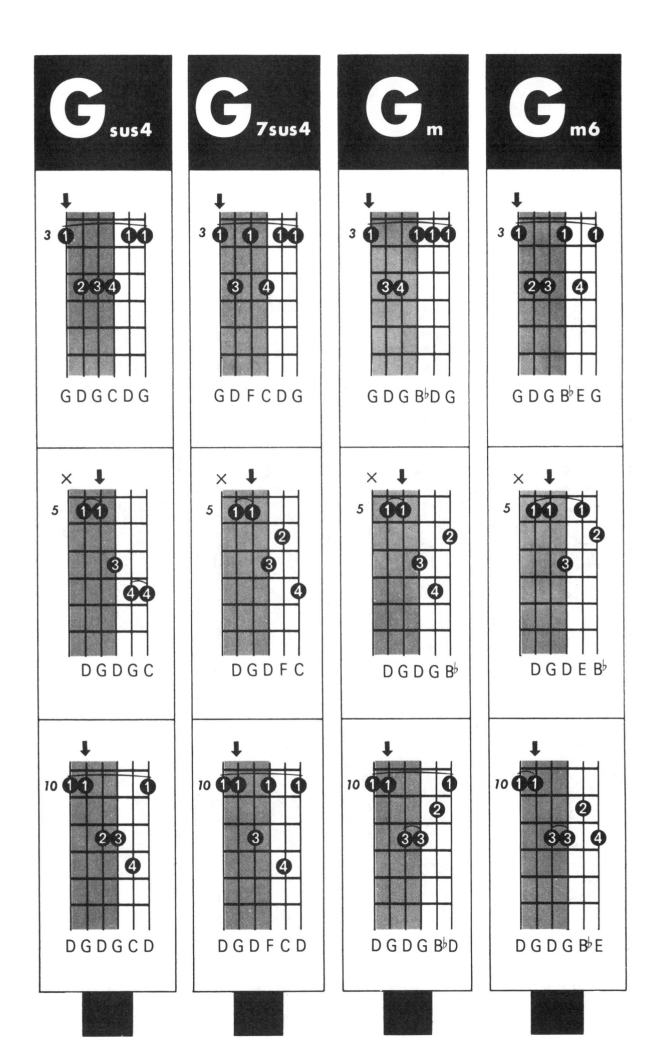

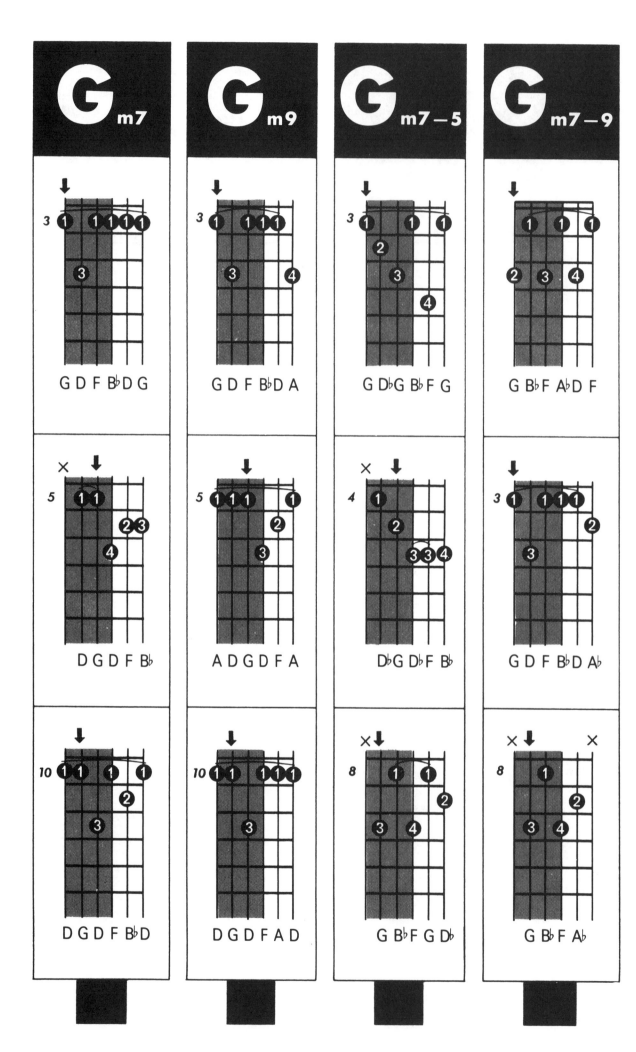

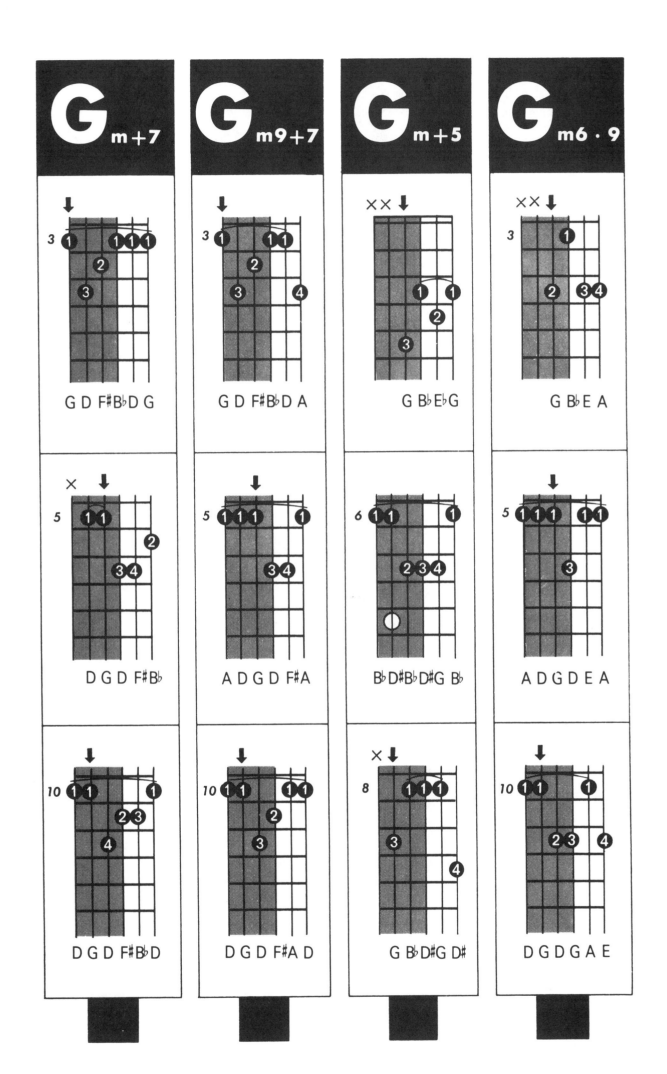

G m+7   G m9+7   G m+5   G m6·9

G m+7

3
G D F#B♭D G

5
D G D F#B♭

10
D G D F#B♭D

G m9+7

3
G D F#B♭D A

5
A D G D F#A

10
D G D F#A D

G m+5

××
G B♭E♭G

6
B♭D#B♭D#G B♭

8
×
G B♭D#G D#

G m6·9

××
G B♭E A

5
A D G D E A

10
D G D G A E

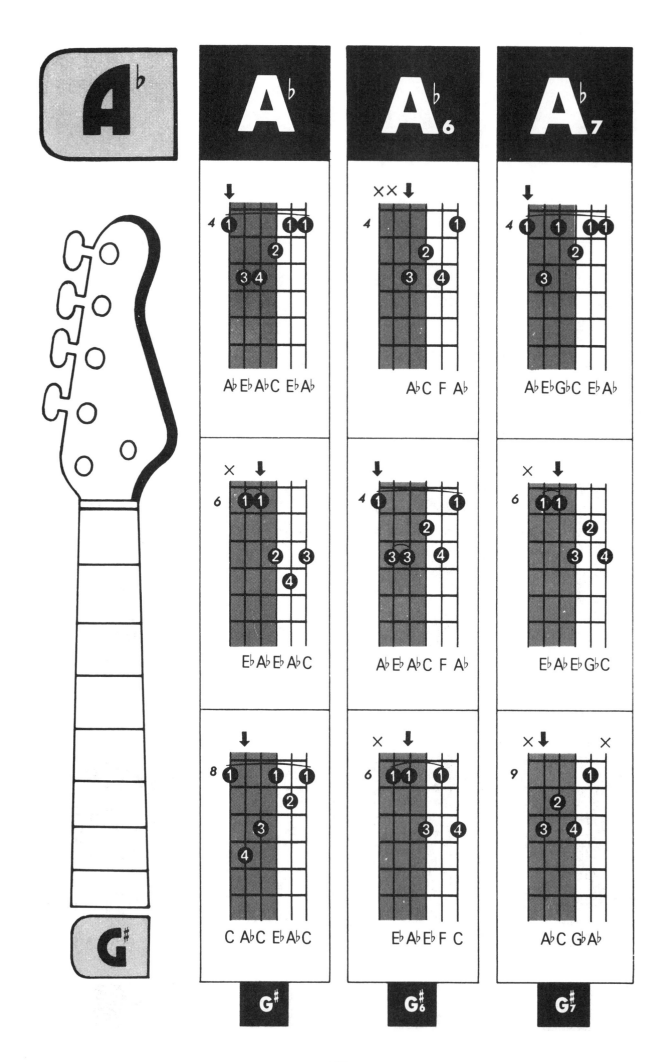

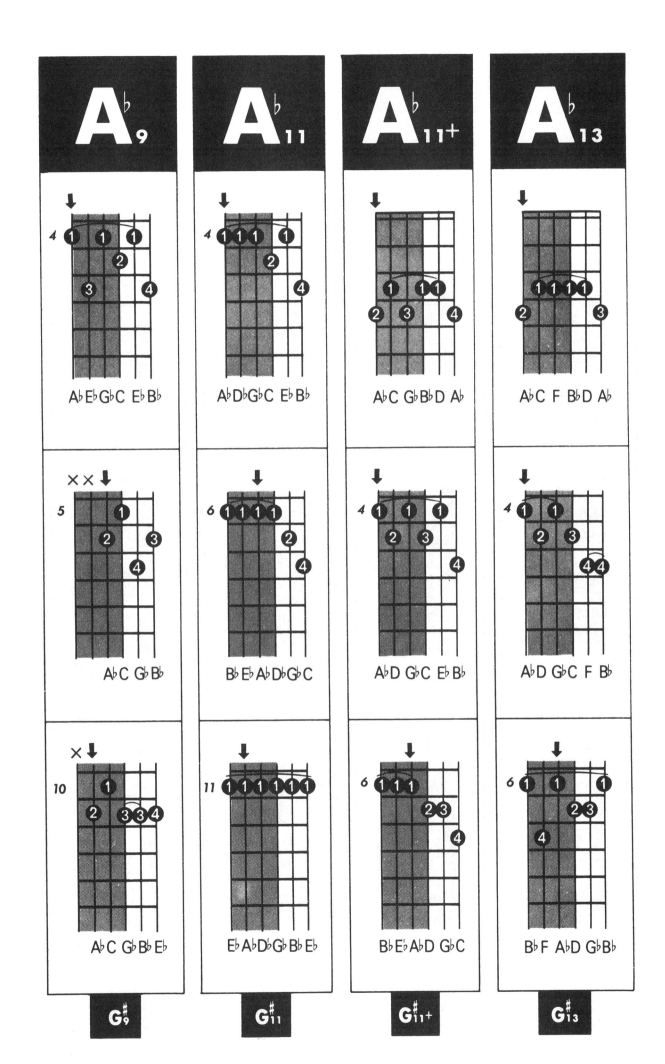

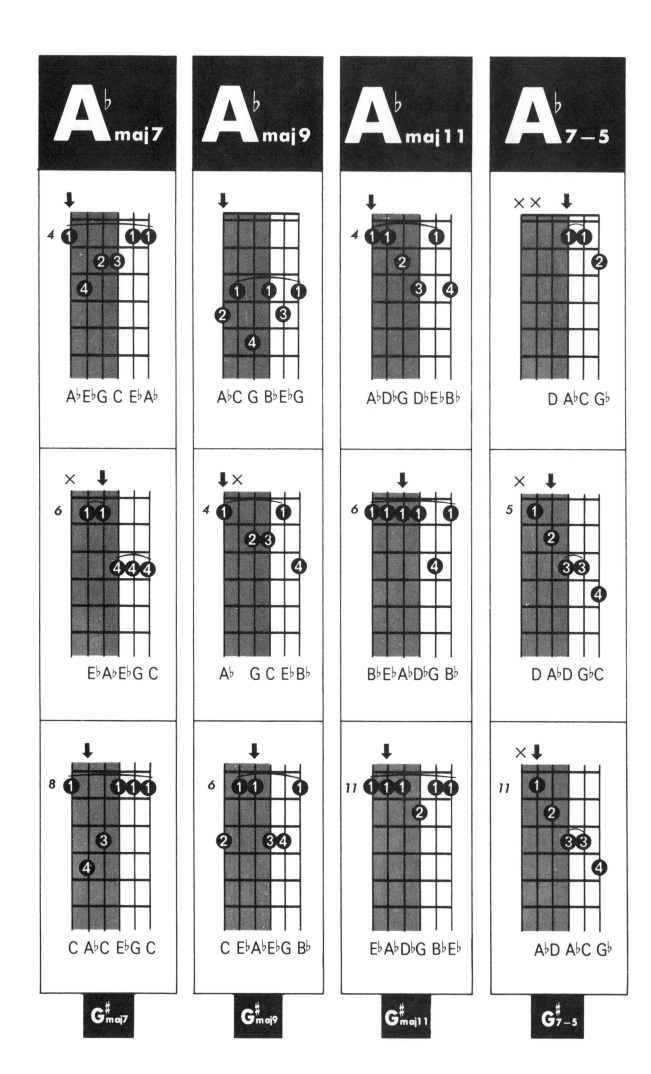

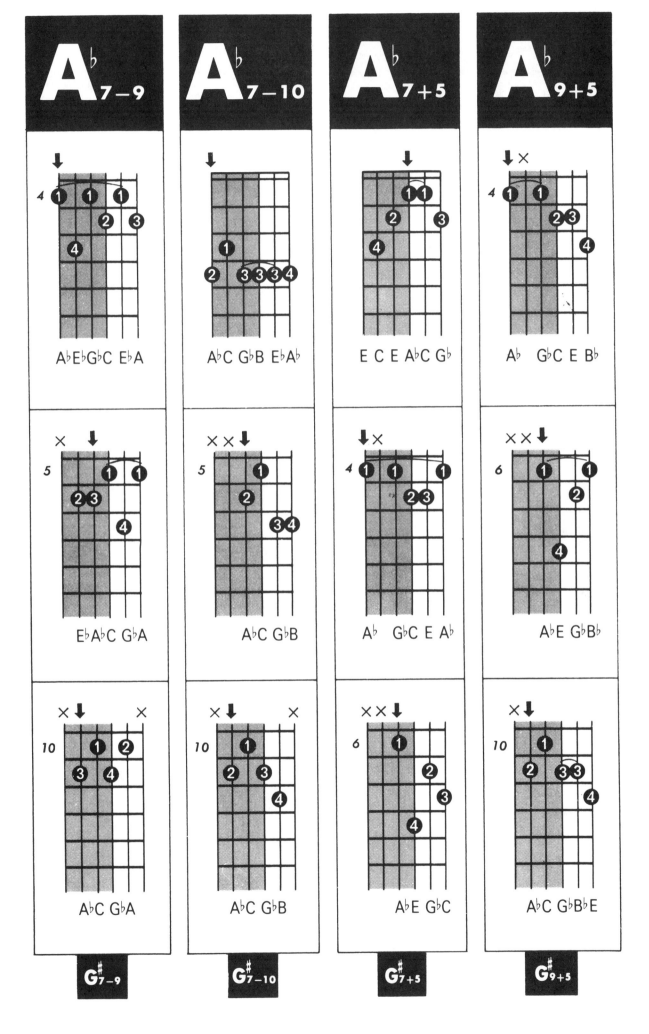

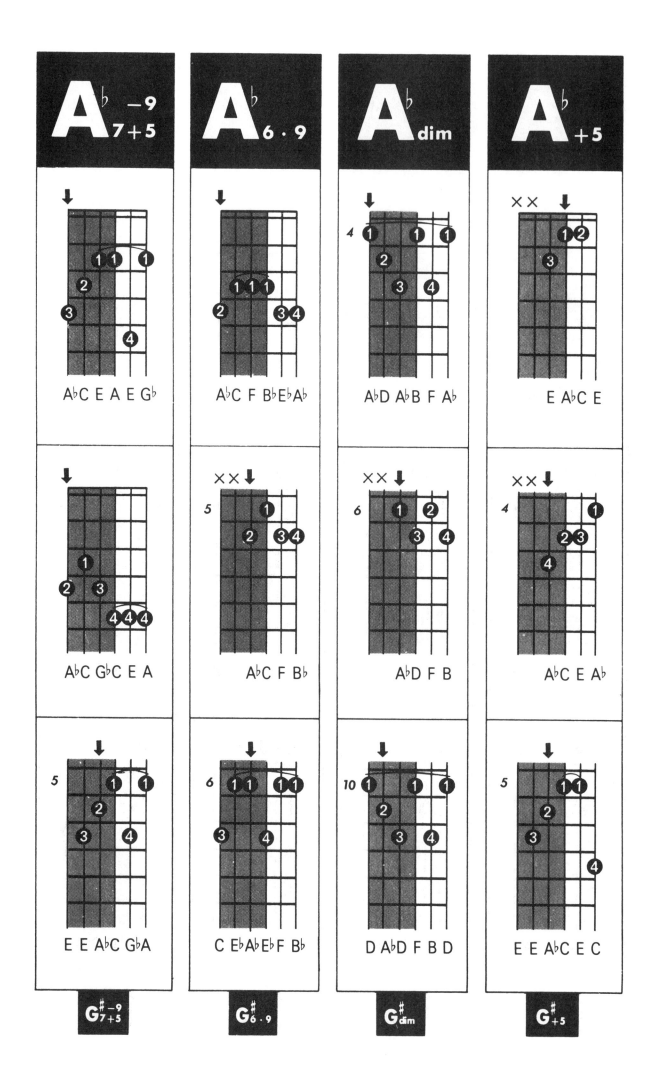

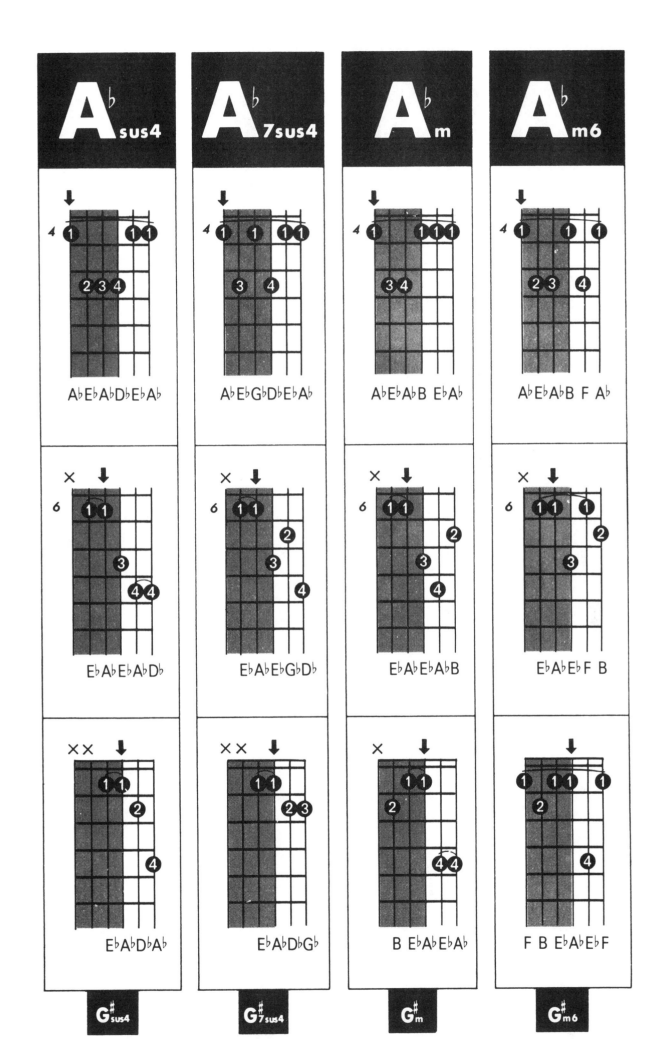

A♭sus4

A♭E♭A♭D♭E♭A♭

E♭A♭E♭A♭D♭

E♭A♭D♭A♭

G#sus4

A♭7sus4

A♭E♭G♭D♭E♭A♭

E♭A♭E♭G♭D♭

E♭A♭D♭G♭

G#7sus4

A♭m

A♭E♭A♭B E♭A♭

E♭A♭E♭A♭B

B E♭A♭E♭A♭

G#m

A♭m6

A♭E♭A♭B F A♭

E♭A♭E♭F B

F B E♭A♭E♭F

G#m6

A♭

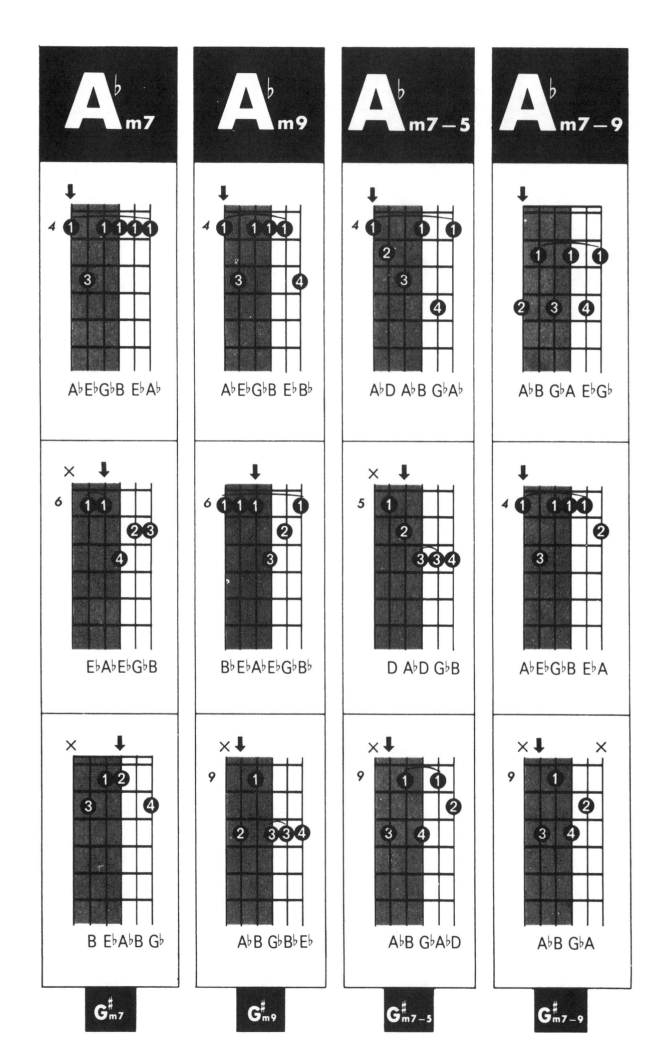

78

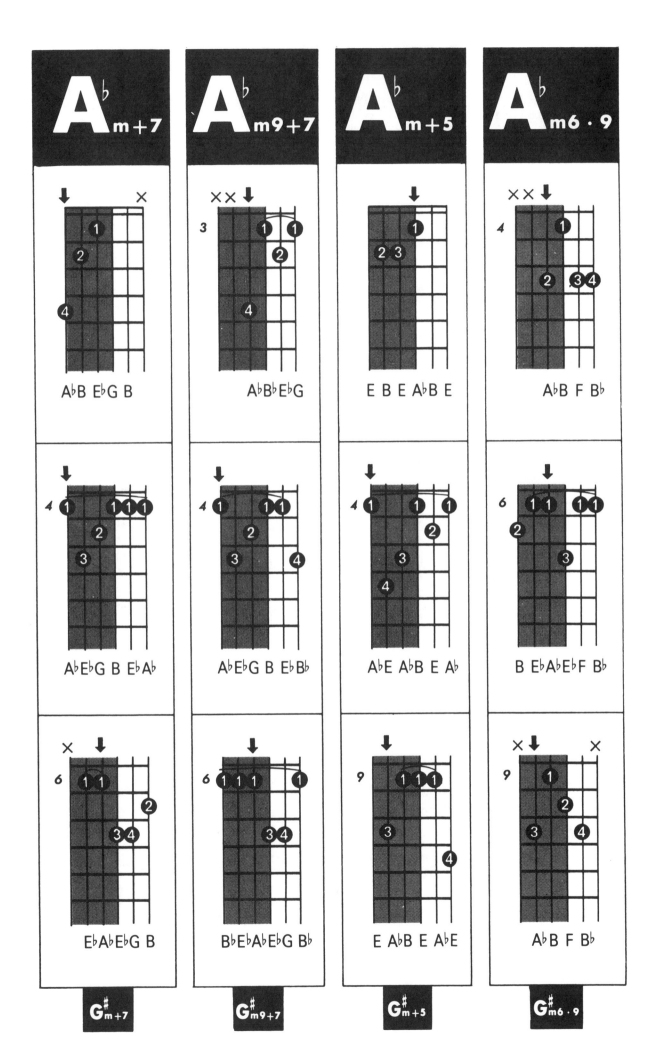

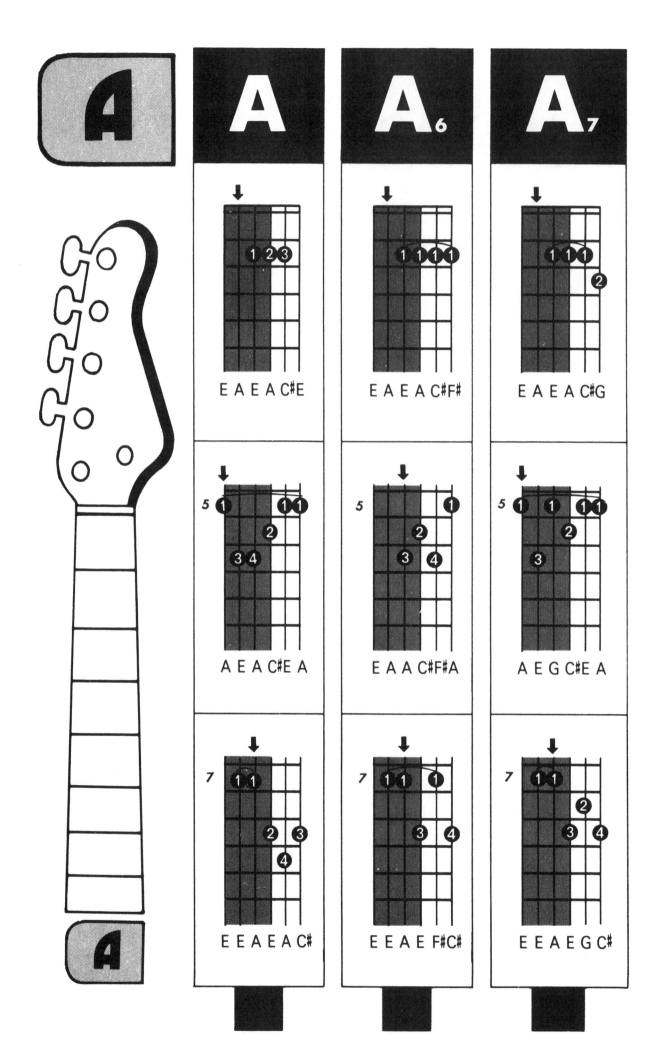

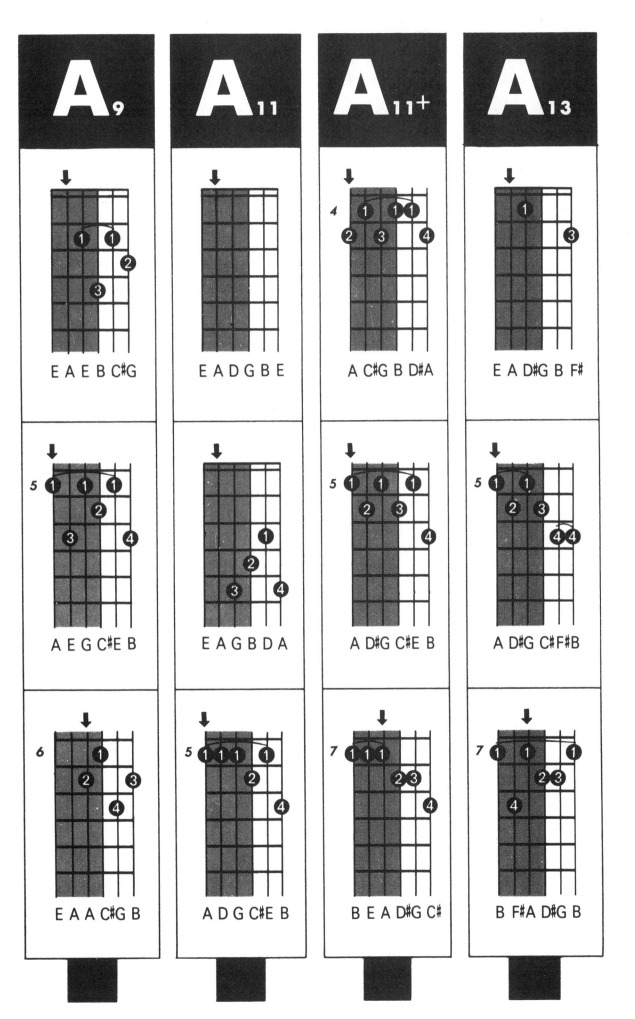

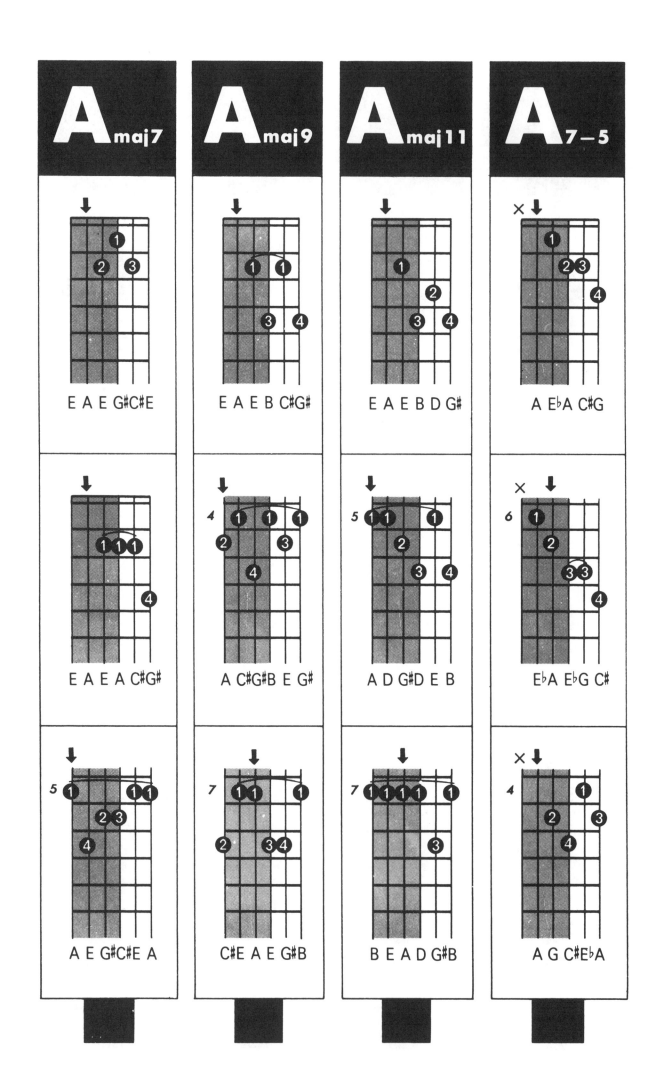

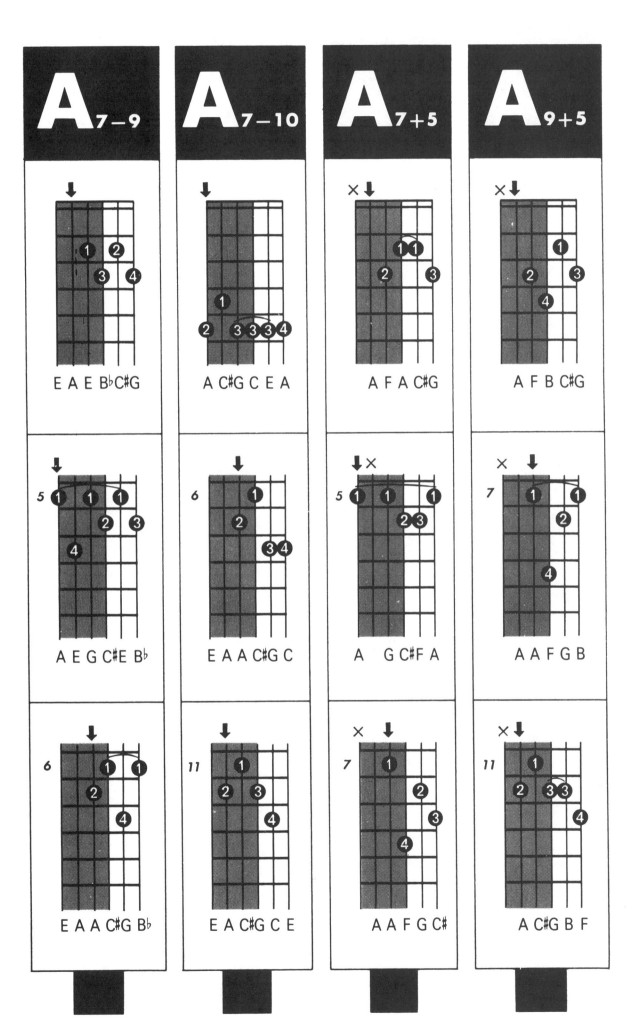

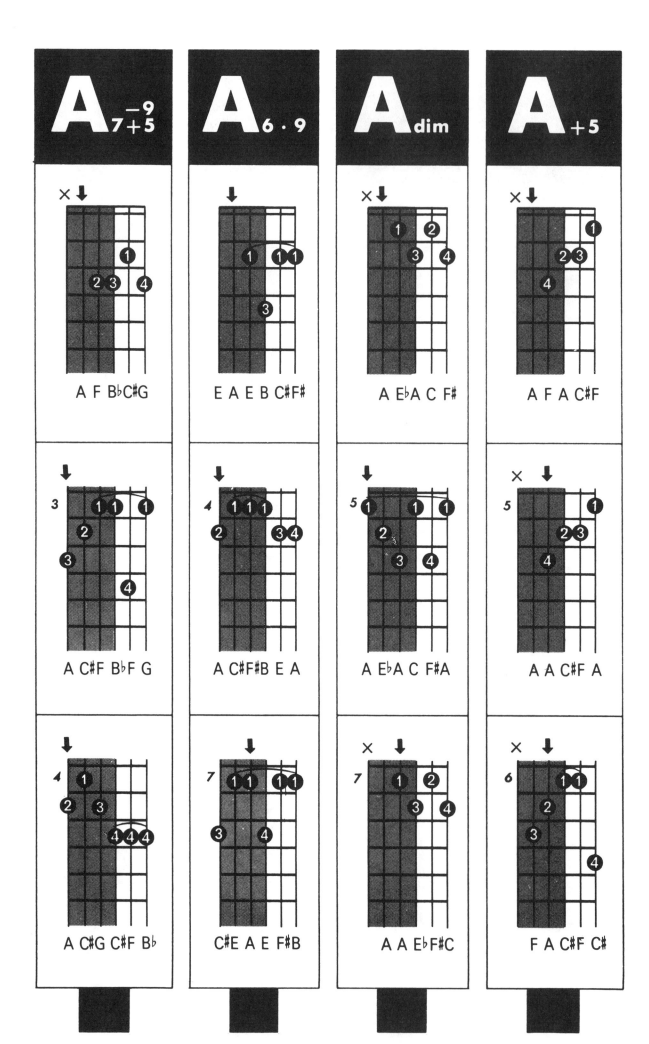

A$_{7+5}^{-9}$ A F B♭C#G   A C#F B♭F G   A C#G C#F B♭

A$_{6\cdot9}$ E A E B C#F#   A C#F#B E A   C#E A E F#B

A$_{dim}$ A E♭A C F#   A E♭A C F#A   A A E♭F#C

A$_{+5}$ A F A C#F   A A C#F A   F A C#F C#

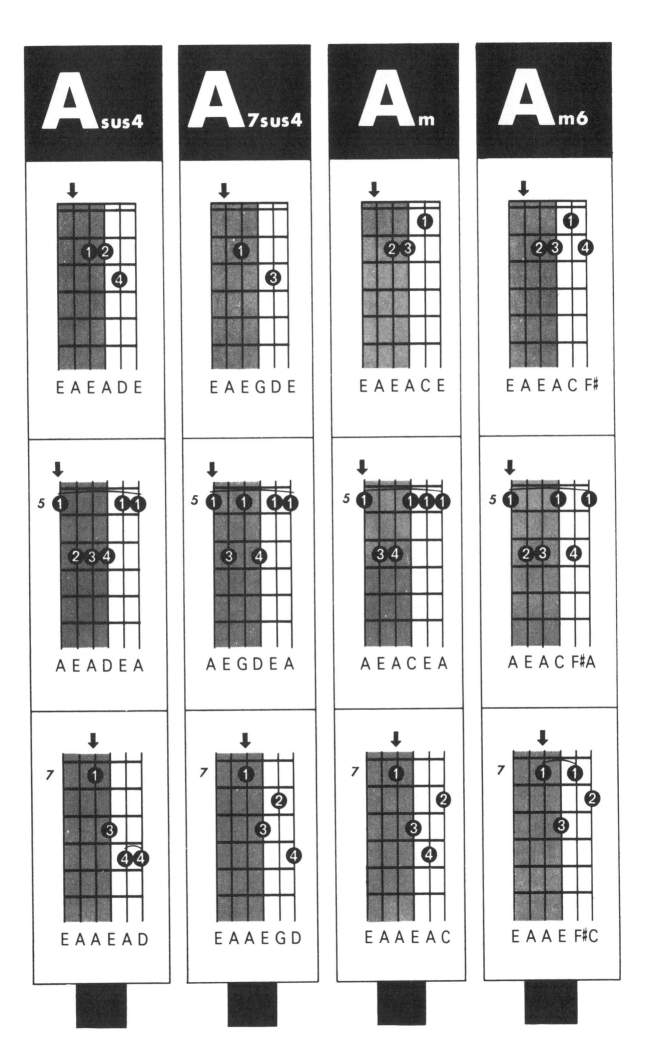

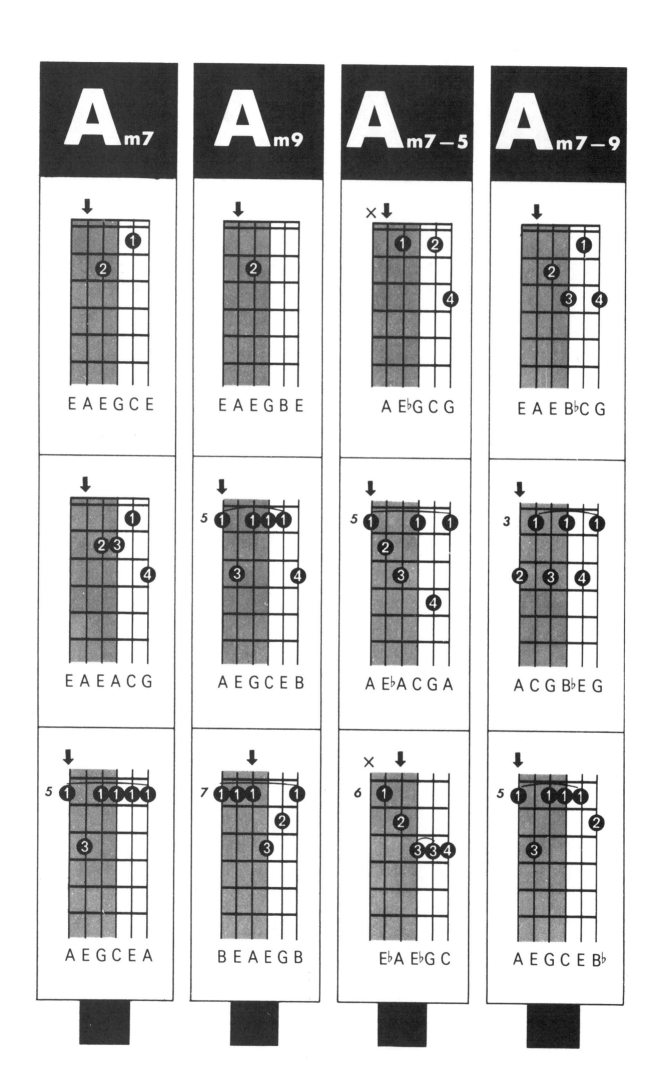

Am7   **A**m9   **A**m7–5   **A**m7–9

E A E G C E   E A E G B E   A E♭G C G   E A E B♭C G

E A E A C G   A E G C E B   A E♭A C G A   A C G B♭E G

A E G C E A   B E A E G B   E♭A E♭G C   A E G C E B♭

Mighty To Save

Words and Music by Reuben Morgan and Ben Fielding

Intro: Guitar Pick/ Gus+thing 2measures/ 2measures / Verse I / Ch. 1x / Intro / V2 / Chorus 2x / Bridge - Music Interlude then "Shine"
4 measures   4 measures

Verse 1   Guitar Pick/ Keyboard chords Drums in   Chorus - 2x.   Bridge - Shine

End on D.

```
C                        G
   Everyone needs com-passion
                  Em
Love that's never failing
       D          C
Let mercy fall on me
                         G
Everyone needs for-giveness
                  Em
The kindness of a Saviour
       D          C      D      C    D
The hope of na-tions
```

(1st time
  Bass Guitar 1st note
  Acoustic guitar)

```
Chorus    1st time 1x.    2nd time 2x.
G                            D
Saviour He can move the mountains
           C          G
My God is mighty to save
      Em        D
He is mighty to save
      G                  D
For-ever Author of sal-vation
                 C          G
He rose and conquered the grave
      Em            D
Jesus conquered the grave
```

(Intro; All in (Bass 1st note) then verse 2)   1st time

Bridge Music Interlude C G / D, Em ||

```
Verse 2                    C                  G                  D              Em
So take me as You find me  Shine your light and  let the whole world see   we're sing
All my fears and failures  C          G          D          Em
Fill my life again          For the glory    of the ris-en King    Jesus
I give my life to follow   C                  G                  D              Em
Everything I believe in    Shine your light and  let the whole world see   we're sing
Now I surrender  C O C D   C          G          D
                            For the glory    of the ris-en King
```

Chorus - 1x

Jesus

Chorus 1st time
(Bass Guitar 1st note
Keyboard also.
Guitar Pick

Chorus 2nd time all in

Bridge 1 time - everyone
2nd time voice + drums
3rd time all in

CCLI Song #4591782
©2006 Hillsong Publishing
For use solely with the SongSelect Terms of Use. All rights Reserved. www.ccli.com
CCLI License #215117

Alyssa Perillo
631 428-6047

Like A Fire

Words and Music by **Jonathan Hunt**

Key - C

Verse 1

    Am7   **G**
Like a fire shut up in my bones
                       F   **G**
I want the world to know You are God
          Am7   **G**
With a passion burning deep with-in
                    F   **G**
I want the world to know that You live

Instrumental 1

Am7 **F** **G** **Am7** **F** **G** **Am7** **F** **G** **Dm7** **F**

Verse 2

G   **Am7**   **G**
Let Your presence come and satu-rate
                  F   **G**
Every part of me make me new
         Am7   **G**
Let Your Spirit come and move with-in
                 F   **G**
Fill me once a-gain 'cause I need more

Chorus

           F   **Am7**   **G**
Jesus I'm desperate   for You
          F   **Am7**   **G**
Jesus I'm hungry   for You
          F   **Am7**   **G**
Jesus I'm longing   for You
          Dm7   **Am7** **G**
'Cause Lord You are   all I want

Instrumental 2

F **C** **Am7** **G**

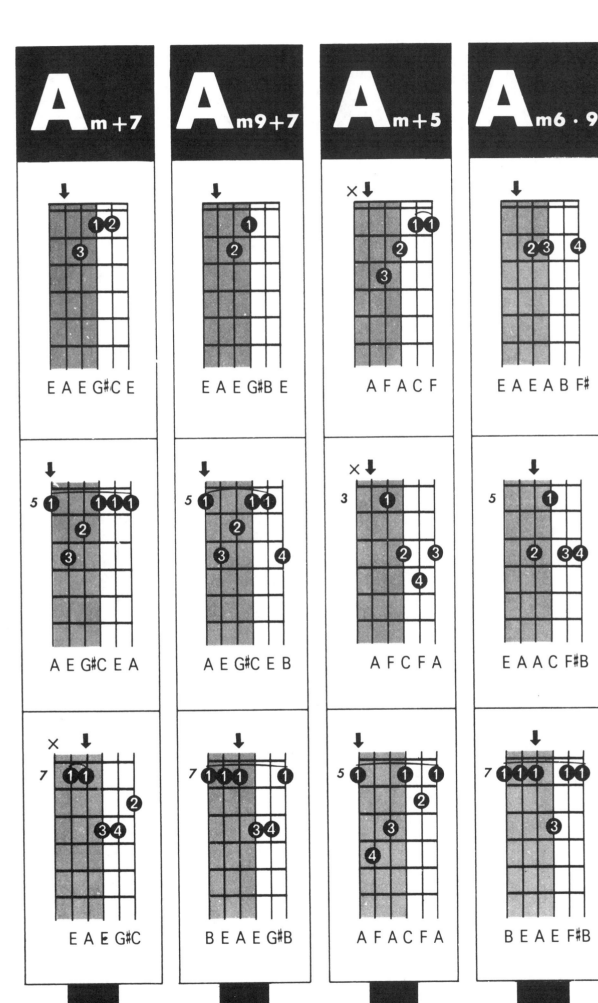

Am+7 · **A**m9+7 · **A**m+5 · **A**m6·9

E A E G#C E · E A E G#B E · A F A C F · E A E A B F#

A E G#C E A · A E G#C E B · A F C F A · E A A C F#B

E A E G#C · B E A E G#B · A F A C F A · B E A E F#B

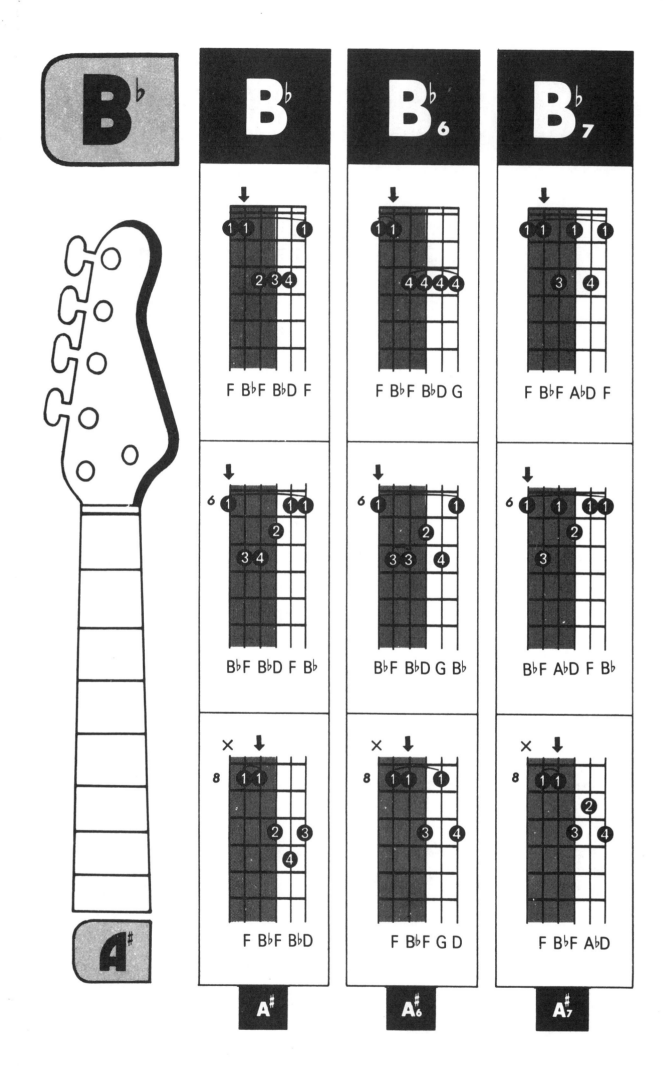

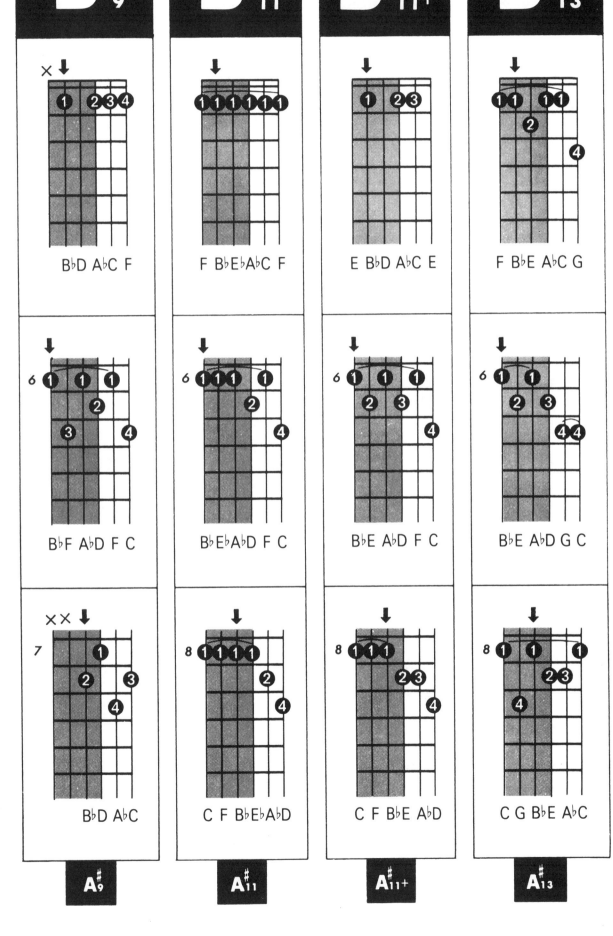

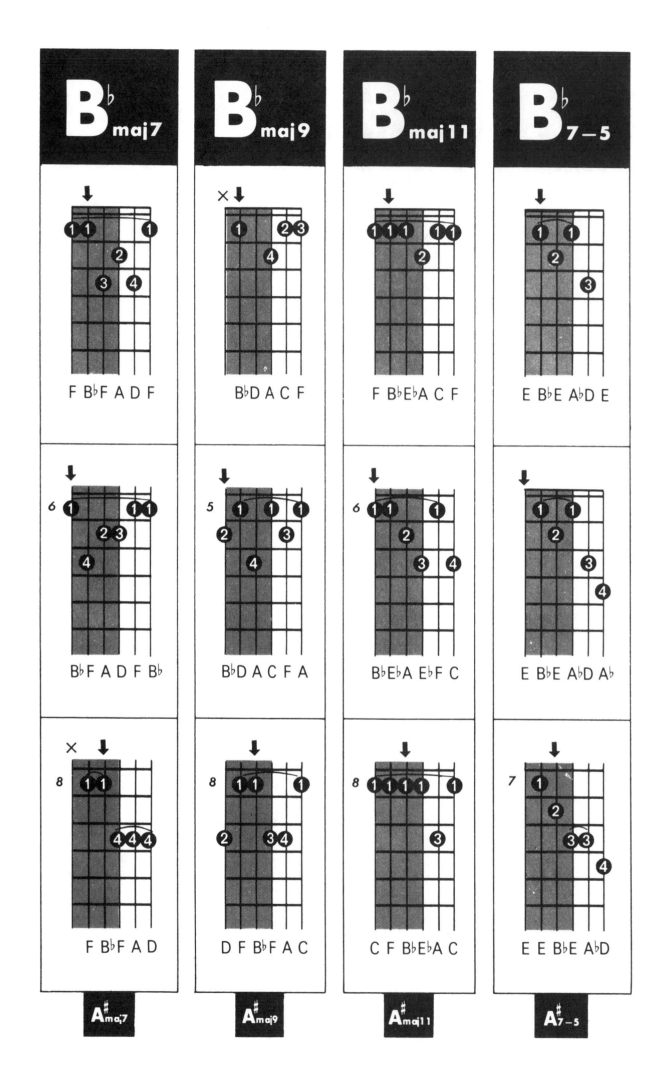

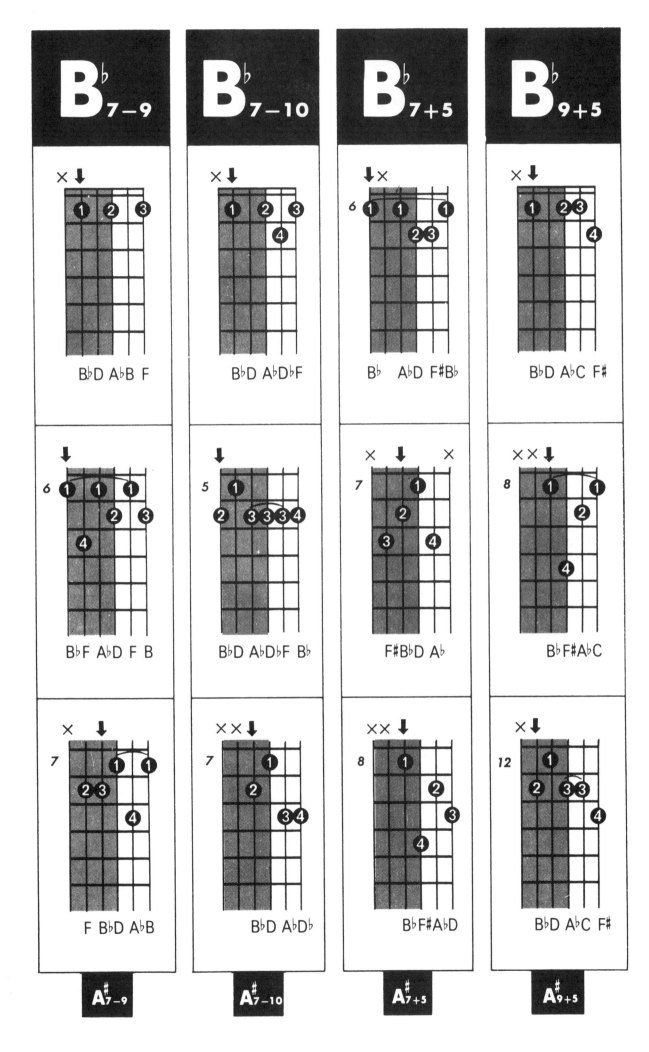

91

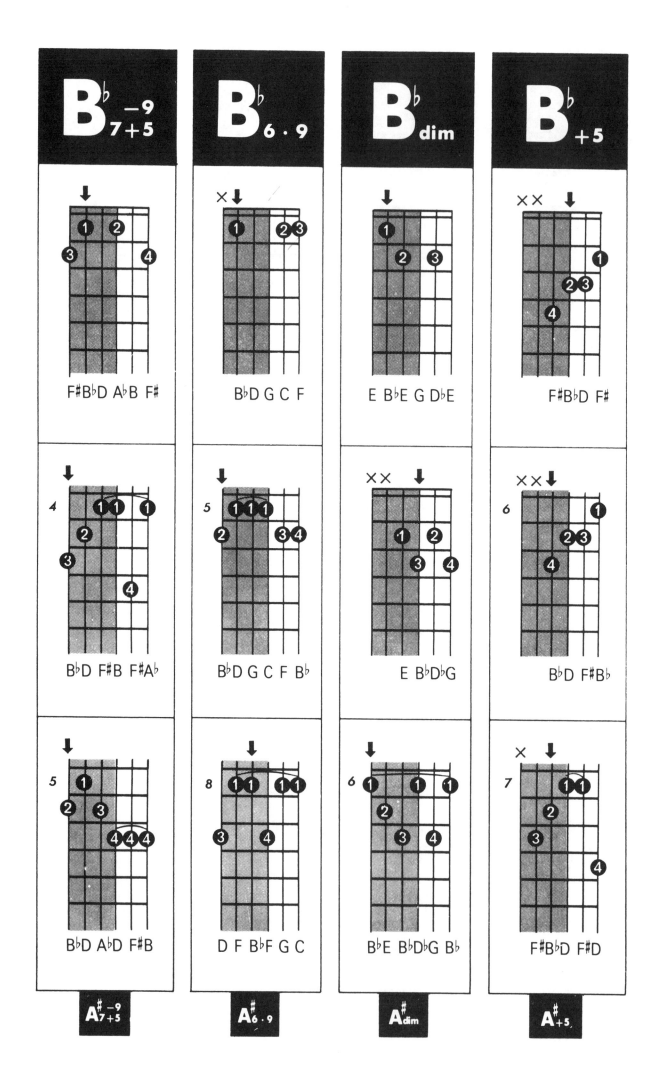

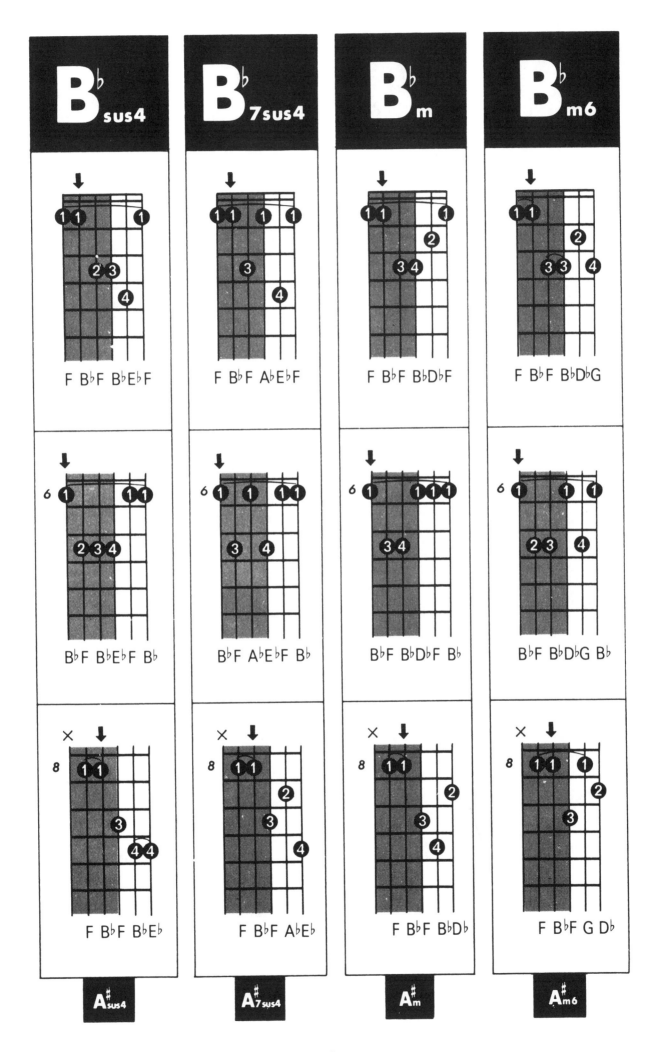

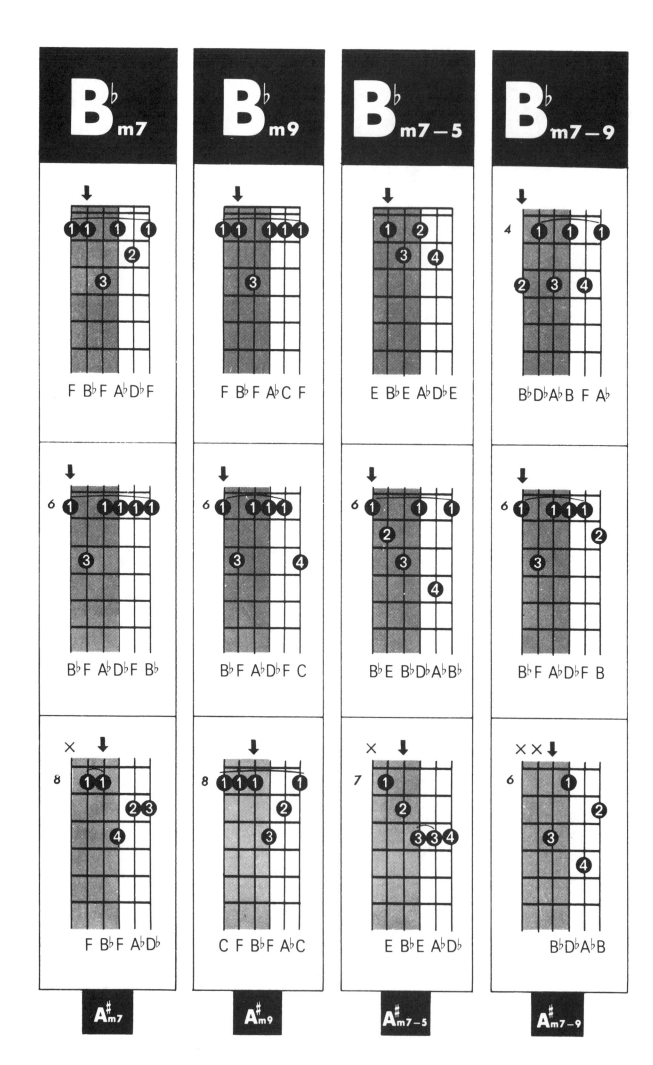

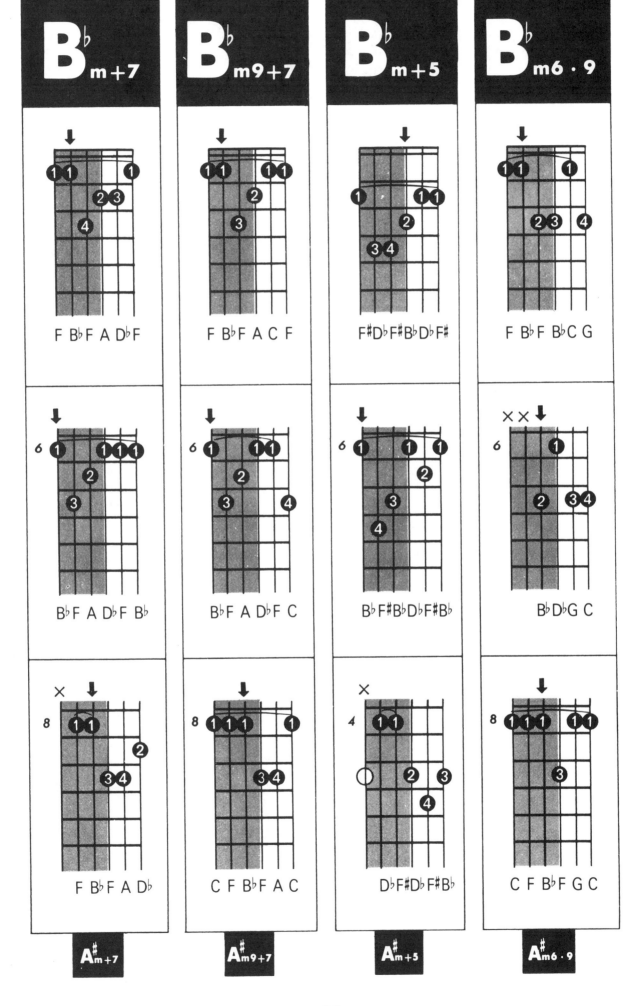

95

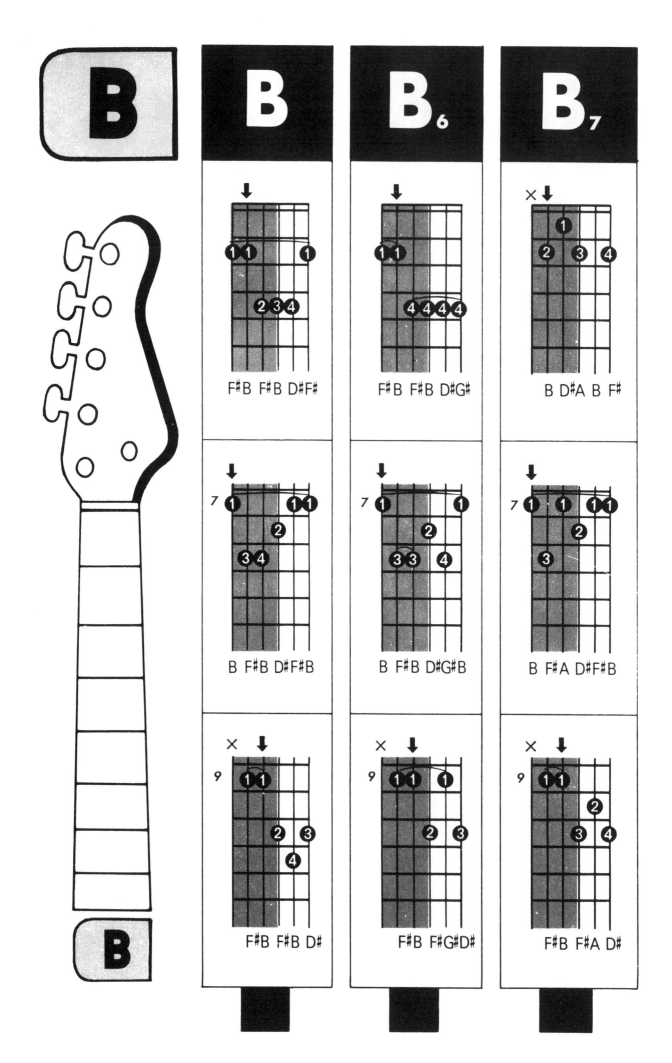

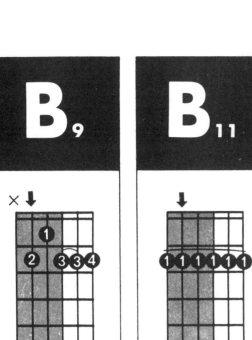

B₉ B₁₁ B₁₁⁺ B₁₃

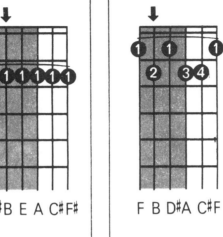

B D#A C#F#   F#B E A C#F#   F B D#A C#F   F#B F A C#G#

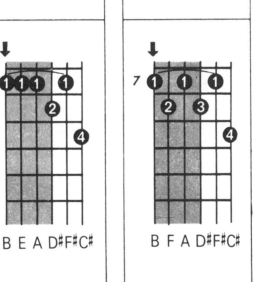
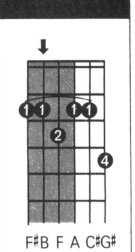

B F#A D#F#C#   B E A D#F#C#   B F A D#F#C#   B D#G#C#F B

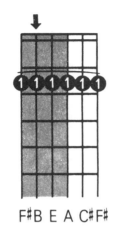
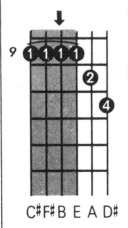
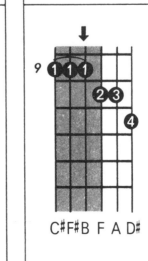
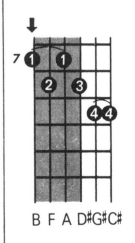

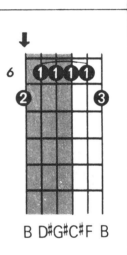

A B D#A C#   C#F#B E A D#   C#F#B F A D#   B F A D#G#C#

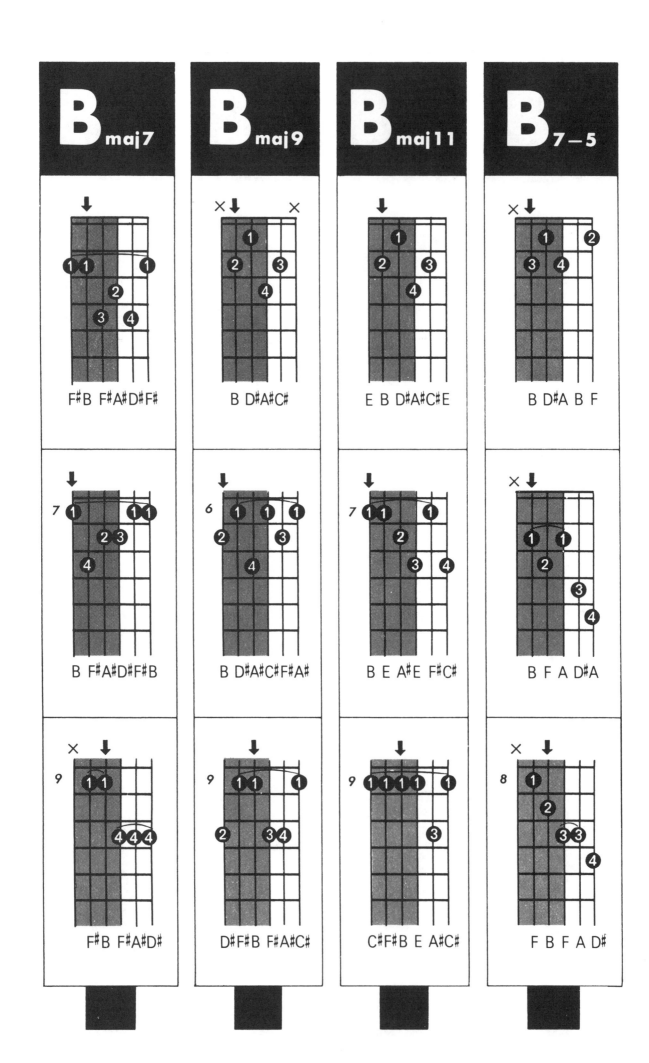

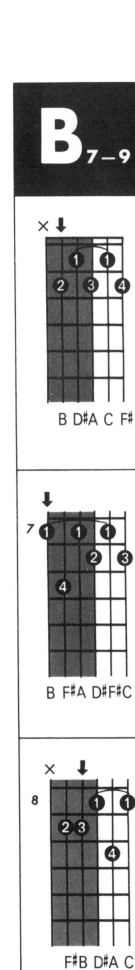

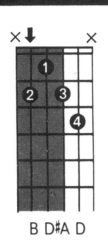

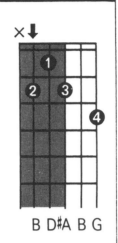

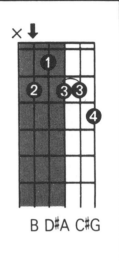

B₇₋₉

B D#A C F#

B F#A D#F#C

F#B D#A C

B₇₋₁₀

B D#A D

B D#A D F#B

A B D#A D

B₇₊₅

B D#A B G

A G B D#A

A B G A D#

B₉₊₅

B D#A C#G

A G C#D#A

B A D#G C#

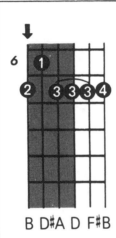
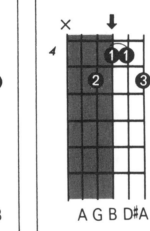
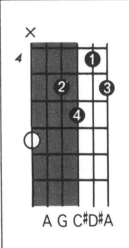
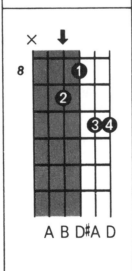
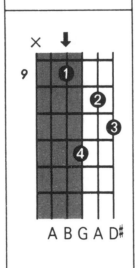
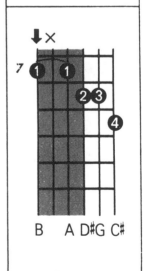

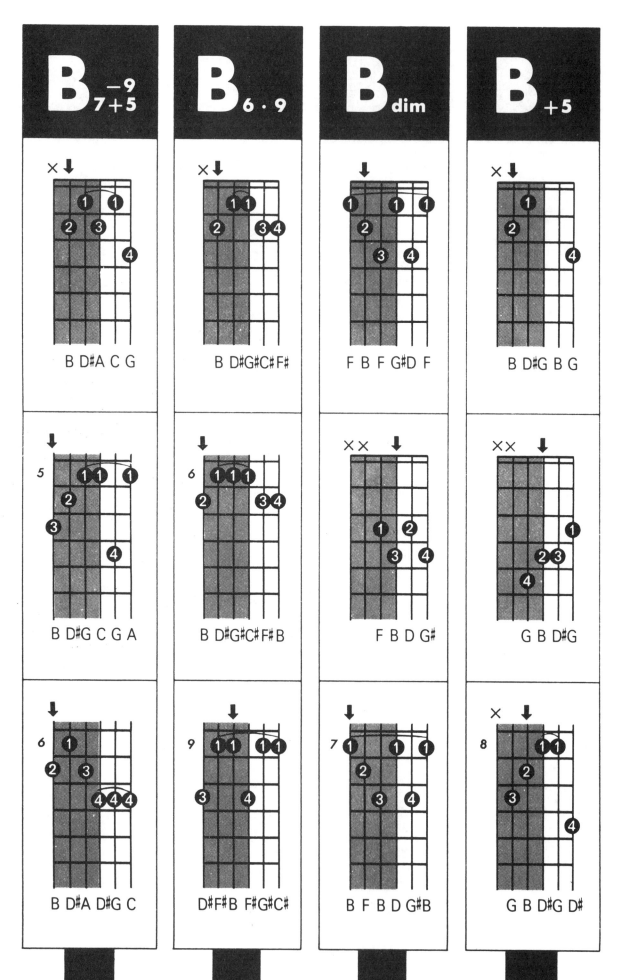

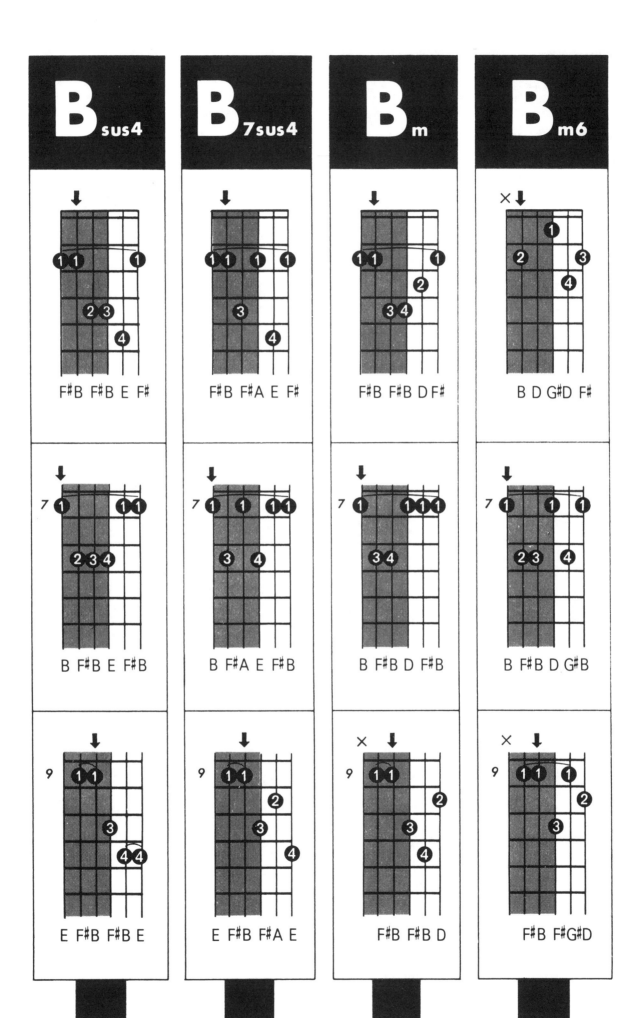

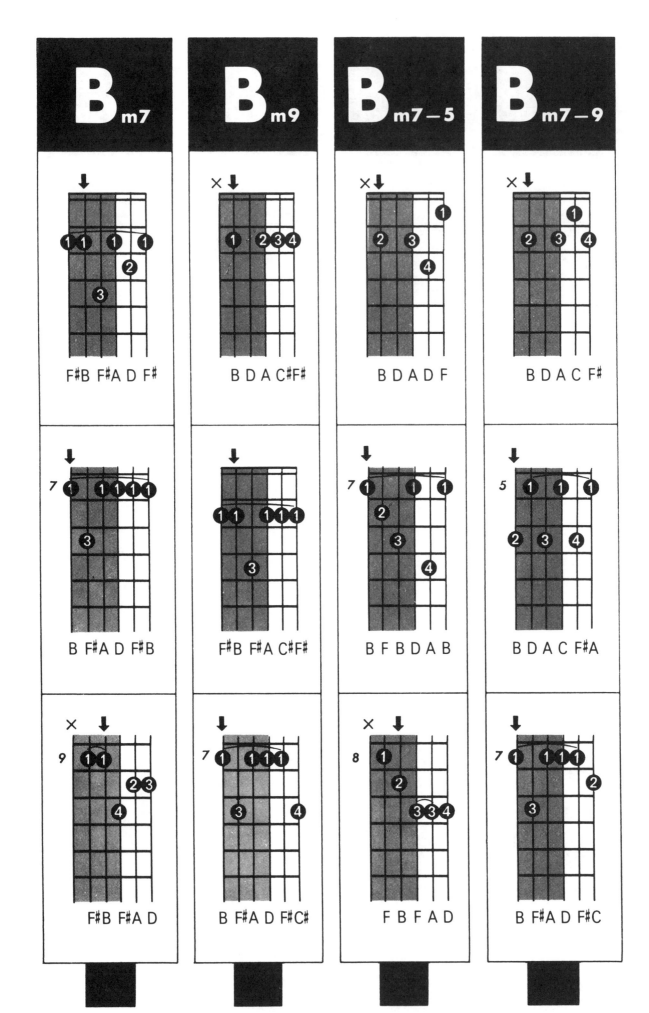

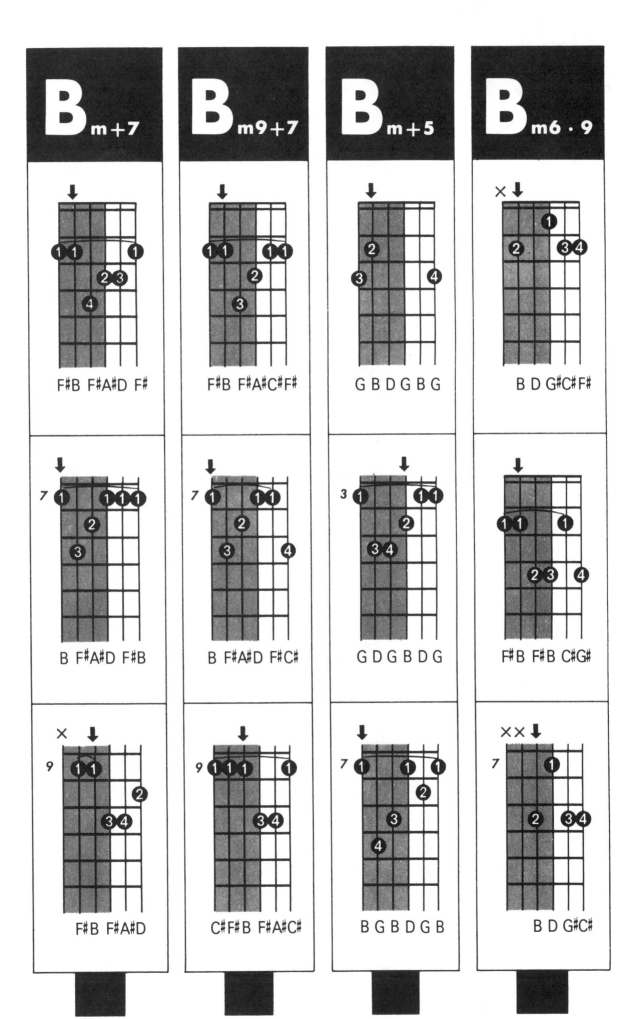

B m+7 B m9+7 B m+5 B m6·9

F#B F#A#D F#

F#B F#A#C#F#

G B D G B G

B D G#C#F#

B F#A#D F#B

B F#A#D F#C#

G D G B D G

F#B F#B C#G#

F#B F#A#D

C#F#B F#A#C#

B G B D G B

B D G#C#

HAL LEONARD GUITAR METHOD

THE HAL LEONARD GUITAR METHOD is designed for anyone just learning to play acoustic or electric guitar. It is based on years of teaching guitar students of all ages, and it also reflects some of the best guitar teaching ideas from around the world.

This comprehensive method is preferred by teachers and students alike for many reasons:

- Learning sequence is carefully paced with clear instructions that make it easy to learn

- Popular songs increase the incentive to learn to play

- Versatile enough to be used as self-instruction or with a teacher

- Audio accompaniments let students have fun and sound great while practicing.

BOOK 1

Book 1 provides beginning instruction which includes tuning, playing position, musical symbols, notes in first position, the C, G, G7, D, D7, A7, and Em chords, rhythms through eighth notes, strumming and picking, 100 great songs, riffs, and examples. Added features are a chord chart and a selection of well-known songs, including "Ode to Joy," "Rockin' Robin," "Greensleeves," "Give My Regards to Broadway," and "Time Is on My Side."

00699010 Book........................$5.95
00699027 Book/CD Pack.........................$9.95

BOOK 2

Book 2 continues the instruction started in Book 1 and covers: Am, Dm, A, E, F and B7 chords; power chords; fingerstyle guitar; syncopations, dotted rhythms, and triplets; Carter style solos; bass runs; pentatonic scales; improvising; tablature; 92 great songs, riffs and examples; notes in first and second position; and more! The CD includes 57 full-band tracks for demonstration or play-along.

00699020 Book...........................$5.95
00697313 Book/CD Pack..........................$9.95

BOOK 3

Book 3 covers: the major, minor, pentatonic, and chromatic scales, sixteenth notes; barre chords; drop D tuning; movable scales; notes in fifth position; slides, hammer-ons, pull-offs, and string bends; chord construction; gear; 90 great songs, riffs, and examples; and more! The CD includes 61 full-band tracks for demonstration or play-along.

00699030 Book........................$5.95
00697316 Book/CD Pack..........................$9.95

COMPOSITE

Books 1, 2, and 3 bound together in an easy-to-use spiral binding.
00699040 Book..........................$14.95

HAL LEONARD GUITAR METHOD VIDEO AND DVD

FOR THE BEGINNING ELECTRIC OR ACOUSTIC GUITARIST
00697318 DVD.............................$19.95
00320159 VHS Videos.............................$14.95

EASY POP RHYTHMS

Strum along with your favorite hits from the Beatles, the Rolling Stones, the Eagles and more!
00697336 Book....................$5.95
00697309 Book/CD Pack....$12.95

MORE EASY POP RHYTHMS

00697338 Book $5.95
00697322 Book/CD Pack.........................$14.95

EVEN MORE EASY POP RHYTHMS

00697340 Book.......................................$5.95
00697323 Book/CD Pack...........................$14.95

EASY POP MELODIES

Play along with your favorite hits from the Beatles, Elton John, Elvis Presley, the Police, Nirvana, and more!
00697281 Book $5.95
00697268 Book/CD Pack...........................$14.95

MORE EASY POP MELODIES

00697280 Book $5.95
00697269 Book/CD Pack...........................$14.95

EVEN MORE EASY POP MELODIES

00699154 Book $5.95
00697270 Book/CD Pack...........................$14.95

BLUES GUITAR

by Greg Koch
This book teaches the basics of blues guitar in the style of B.B. King, Stevie Ray Vaughan, Buddy Guy, Muddy Waters, and more.

00697326 Book/CD Pack....$12.95

COUNTRY GUITAR

by Greg Koch
This book teaches the basics of country guitar in the styles of Chet Atkins, Albert Lee, Merle Travis and more.

00697337 Book/CD Pack....$12.95

JAZZ GUITAR

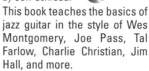

by Jeff Schroedl
This book teaches the basics of jazz guitar in the style of Wes Montgomery, Joe Pass, Tal Farlow, Charlie Christian, Jim Hall, and more.

00695359 Book/CD Pack....$12.95

ROCK GUITAR

by Michael Mueller
This book teaches the basics of rock guitar in the style of Eric Clapton, the Beatles, the Rolling Stones, and many others.
00697319 Book/CD Pack.....$12.95

INCREDIBLE CHORD FINDER

AN EASY-TO-USE GUIDE TO OVER 1,100 GUITAR CHORDS
00697200 6" x 9" Edition $4.95
00697208 9" x 12" Edition $5.95

INCREDIBLE SCALE FINDER

AN EASY-TO-USE GUIDE TO OVER 1,300 GUITAR SCALES
00695568 6" x 9" Edition $4.95
00695490 9" x 12" Edition $5.95

FOR MORE INFORMATION, SEE YOUR LOCAL MUSIC DEALER, OR WRITE TO:

HAL•LEONARD®
CORPORATION
7777 W. BLUEMOUND RD. P.O. BOX 13819 MILWAUKEE, WI 53213

www.halleonard.com